Dead Sea Scrolls Psalms

CW01475902

Dead Sea Scroll

By Thomas P. Miller

Dead Sea Scrolls Psalms

# Dead Sea Scrolls Psalms

### By Thomas P. Miller

# Dead Sea Scrolls Psalms

\*
\*     \*

# INTRODUCTION

This book is a collection of Psalms from the King James Version of the Bible, a collection of Psalms which parallel Psalms which were found within the Dead Sea Scrolls. Not all of the Psalms in the modern Bible were found within the Dead Sea Scrolls, presumably due to the fragmentary condition of the Dead Sea Scrolls. However, it is possible that the original Dead Sea Scrolls had never contained all the Psalms that exist in the modern Hebrew Bible. It is possible that the surviving Dead Sea Scrolls had originally contained only a particular selection out of all the Psalms, perhaps a selection based upon particular theological or political considerations of the sectarians who wrote the Dead Sea Scrolls manuscripts.

This book is **not** a transcription or a translation of the actual Hebrew text of the Dead Sea Scrolls Psalms, and therefore, a transcription or translation of the actual Hebrew text of the Dead Sea Scrolls Psalms must be sought elsewhere in scholarly publications.

The English translation King James Version of the Psalms within this book will only approximate the actual Hebrew text or English translation of the Dead Sea Scrolls Psalms.

The Dead Sea Scrolls Psalms were found within a scroll and fragments of several scrolls which collectively were found within several different caves near to the Dead Sea, and near to the ancient small settlement known as Qumran. One scroll contains the largest collection of Psalm fragments, the scroll numbered as 11Q5, which was found in Cave 11. Several other caves contained scroll fragments which contained fragments of various Psalms. Only a few of the Dead Sea Scroll Psalms fragments were found to contain the complete text of an individual Psalm. Most of the Dead Sea Scroll Psalms fragments contained only portions of the individual Psalms, portions ranging in size from a large number of verses, to a small number of verses, or to a fragment of a single verse.

However, the complete text of the King James Version of the individual Psalms found in fragmentary form in the Dead Sea Scrolls will be printed within this book, with the King James Version as an approximate English translation of the Hebrew text of the Dead Sea Scroll **fragments,** with the **fragments** indicated by **bold text** within the printed individual Psalms, according to the **verses** and **fragmented verses** contained within the scroll fragments, **verses** as listed within scholarly reference books. These reference books are listed in the bibliography at the end of this book. These Dead Sea Scroll Psalms **verses** are numbered according to the verse numbering of the Hebrew Bible Psalms, Hebrew Psalms which often have an extra numbered verse for the individual Psalm prologue, a prologue which is not numbered in the English translation Psalms. Therefore, when a Hebrew Psalm has a numbered prologue, as Hebrew verse 1, then Hebrew Psalm verse 2 is the English translation Psalm verse 1, etcetera. The King James Version text used in this book does not contain the individual Psalm prologues, but other text versions which contain the prologues, the prologues are un-numbered in the English translations.

The Dead Sea Scrolls and scroll fragments contain the oldest known manuscript texts of the Hebrew Bible, also known as the Old Testament, and these Dead Sea Scrolls Hebrew Bible manuscript fragments are hundreds of years older than any other known old Hebrew Bible manuscripts. Therefore, whatever differences there may be between the modern standard text of the Hebrew Bible Old Testament and the oldest Hebrew texts found in the Dead Sea Scrolls, there is no way to know how or when any differences arose, between the date of the Dead Sea Scrolls and the date of the modern Hebrew text which is at least hundreds of years later than the Hebrew text of the Dead Sea Scrolls. Furthermore, there is no way to know how or when any Hebrew Bible texts may have been written or existed before the time of the existence of the Dead Sea Scrolls.

However, the actual approximate date when the Dead Sea Scroll Hebrew Bible manuscripts were written is a matter of dispute among scholars. Some scholars may suggest the Dead Sea Scrolls were written as early as the second century before the Christian Era (BCE), and other scholars may suggest that at least some of the Dead Sea Scrolls were written in the first century of the Christian Era (CE), perhaps during the lifetime of Jesus the Nazarene, or perhaps sometime shortly before 70 AD and the destruction of Jerusalem, when the Roman army defeated the Jews in the Jewish War. Most scholars agree that the Dead Sea Scrolls were written sometime before 70 AD, although a few scholars may suggest a time as late as the early second century of the Christian Era.

Since the Dead Sea Scrolls manuscript texts of the Psalms and other books of the Hebrew Bible are frequently fragmentary and thus smaller or shorter than modern Hebrew Bible texts, it may be possible that the original autograph texts were originally smaller or shorter, and that later writers added to the original texts, thus later expanding the texts into the length of the modern texts. Verse numbering did not and does not exist within the Dead Sea Scrolls, and the current modern verse numbering of the Hebrew Bible text and the Dead Sea Scrolls texts is a much later development in Bible text history.

The Dead Sea Scrolls, as a large collection of scrolls and fragments, contain sectarian original writings manuscripts and scroll fragments, in addition to Hebrew Bible Scroll manuscripts and fragments. Some of these sectarian manuscripts contain references to someone known as the Teacher of Righteousness, however, the actual identity of the Teacher of Righteousness is unknown, and various scholars have suggested various historical persons as possibly being the Teacher of Righteousness.

It may be possible that the Teacher of Righteousness was the author of some of the sectarian Dead Sea Scrolls. It may be possible that the Teacher of Righteousness was the author of some of the Dead Sea Scrolls Psalms, or perhaps the Teacher of Righteousness was a writer who added verses to earlier existing Psalms.

Some scholars have suggested that the Teacher of Righteousness was John the Baptist. Some scholars have suggested that the Teacher of Righteousness was Jesus the Nazarene. Some scholars have suggested that the Teacher of Righteousness was James the Righteous, also known as Jacob, the most famous younger brother of Jesus the Nazarene.

If some portion of the Dead Sea Scrolls Psalms were written by Jesus the Nazarene, it would seem that some of the Dead Sea Scrolls Psalms were written before the crucifixion of Jesus the Nazarene, and it would seem that some of the Dead Sea Scrolls Psalms were written after the crucifixion and resurrection of Jesus the Nazarene.

Only the Psalms found in the Dead Sea Scrolls are included in this book. The King James Version of the Psalms as printed in this book has been slightly modified by the editor, Thomas P. Miller.

Dead Sea Scrolls or fragments are identified by cave number - Q - collection number.

Small portions of the Dead Sea Scrolls Psalms texts that are by scholars identified by scroll column number, or scroll fragment number, within the collection number, these fragment identification numbers are not included in this book for the detailed identification of the manuscript fragments. These fragment numbers are not the same as the verse numbers, but the verse numbers are listed in association with the fragment numbers. The detailed identification of the fragment numbers are found in the two volumes of the reference books listed in the bibliography at the end of this book.

## Psalm 2                    11Q7 & 3Q2

**Psalm 2:1 Why do the heathen rage, and the people imagine a vain thing?**
**2:2 The kings of the earth set themselves, and the rulers take counsel together, against the LORD, and against his anointed, saying,**
**2:3 Let us break their bands asunder, and cast away their cords from us.**
**2:4 He that is seated in the heavens shall laugh: the LORD shall have them in derision.**
**2:5 Then shall he speak unto them in his wrath, and vex them in his sore displeasure.**
**2:6 Yet have I set my king upon my holy hill of Zion.**
**2:7 I will declare the decree: the LORD hath said unto me, Thou art my Son; this day have I begotten thee.**
**2:8 Ask of me, and I shall give thee the heathen for thine inheritance, and the uttermost parts of the earth for thy possession.**
**2:9** Thou shalt break them with a rod of iron; thou shalt dash them in pieces like a potter's vessel.
**2:10** Be wise now therefore, O ye kings: be instructed, ye judges of the earth.
**2:11** Serve the LORD with fear, and rejoice with trembling.
**2:12** Kiss the Son, lest he be angry, and ye perish from the way, when his wrath is kindled but a little. Blessed are all they that put their trust in him.

## Psalm 5     4 Q98(b) & 4Q83

**Psalm 5:1** Give ear to my words, O LORD, consider my meditation. **5:2** Hearken unto the voice of my cry, my King, and my God: for unto thee will I pray.

**5:3** My voice shalt thou hear in the morning, O LORD; in the morning will I direct my prayer unto thee, and will look up.

**5:4** For thou art not a God that hath pleasure in wickedness: neither shall evil dwell with thee.

**5:5** The foolish shall not stand in thy sight: thou hatest all workers of iniquity.

**5:6** Thou shalt destroy them that speak falsehood: the LORD will abhor the bloody and deceitful man.

**5:7 But as for me, I will come into thy house in the multitude of thy mercy: and in thy reverence will I worship toward thy holy temple.**

**5:8 Lead me, O LORD, in thy righteousness because of mine enemies; make thy way straight before my face.**

**5:9 For there is no faithfulness in their mouth; their inward part is very wickedness; their throat is an open sepulchre; they flatter with their tongue.**

**5:10 Destroy thou them, O God; let them fall by their own counsels; cast them out in the multitude of their transgressions; for they have rebelled against thee.**

**5:11 But let all those that put their trust in thee rejoice: let them ever shout for joy, because thou defendest them: let them also that love thy name be joyful in thee.**

**5:12 For thou, LORD, wilt bless the righteous; with favour wilt thou compass him as with a shield.**

## Psalm 6        4 Q98(b) & 4Q83 & 11Q8

**Psalm 6:1 O LORD, rebuke me not in thine anger, neither chasten me in thy hot displeasure.**
**6:2 Have mercy upon me, O LORD; for I am weak: O LORD, heal me; for my bones are vexed.**
**6:3 My soul is also sore vexed: but thou, O LORD, how long?**
**6:4** Return, O LORD, deliver my soul: oh save me for thy mercies' sake.
**6:5** For in death there is no remembrance of thee: in the grave who shall give thee thanks?
**6:6** I am weary with my groaning; all the night make I my bed to swim; I water my couch with my tears.
**6:7** Mine eye is consumed because of grief; it waxeth old because of all mine enemies.
**6:8** Depart from me, all ye workers of iniquity; for the LORD hath heard the voice of my weeping.
**6:9** The LORD hath heard my supplication; the LORD will receive my prayer.
**6:10** Let all mine enemies be ashamed and sore vexed: let them return and be ashamed suddenly.

## Psalm 9        11Q7 & 11Q8

**Psalm 9:1** I will praise thee, O LORD, with my whole heart; I will show forth all thy marvellous works.

**9:2 I will be glad and rejoice in thee: I will sing praise to thy name, O thou most High.**

**9:3 When mine enemies are turned back, they shall fall and perish at thy presence.**

**9:4 For thou hast maintained my right and my cause; thou sat in the throne judging right.**

**9:5 Thou hast rebuked the heathen, thou hast destroyed the wicked, thou hast blotted out their name for ever and ever.**

**9:6 O thou enemy, destructions are come to a perpetual end: and thou hast destroyed cities; their memorial is perished with them.**

**9:7** But the LORD shall endure for ever: he hath prepared his throne for judgment.

**9:8** And he shall judge the world in righteousness, he shall minister judgment to the people in uprightness.

**9:9** The LORD also will be a refuge for the oppressed, a refuge in times of trouble.

**9:10** And they that know thy name will put their trust in thee: for thou, LORD, hast not forsaken them that seek thee.

**9:11** Sing praises to the LORD, which dwelleth in Zion: declare among the people his doings.

**9:12** When he maketh inquisition for blood, he remembereth them: he forgetteth not the cry of the humble.

**9:13** Have mercy upon me, O LORD; consider my trouble which I suffer of them that hate me, thou that liftest me up from the gates of death:

**9:14** That I may show forth all thy praise in the gates of the daughter of Zion: I will rejoice in thy salvation.

**9:15** The heathen are sunk down in the pit that they made: in the net which they hid is their own foot taken.

**9:16** The LORD is known by the judgment which he executeth: the wicked is snared in the work of his own hands. Higgaion. Selah.

**9:17** The wicked shall be turned into hell, and all the nations that forget God.
**9:18** For the needy shall not always be forgotten: the expectation of the poor shall not perish for ever.
**9:19** Arise, O LORD; let not man prevail: let the heathen be judged in thy sight.
**9:20** Put them in fear, O LORD: that the nations may know themselves to be but men. Selah.

**Psalm 12**         **11Q7**

**Psalm 12:1** Help, LORD; for the godly man ceaseth; for the faithful fail from among the children of men.

**12:2** They speak vanity every one with his neighbour: with flattering lips and with a double heart do they speak.

**12:3** The LORD shall cut off all flattering lips, and the tongue that speaketh proud things:

**12:4 Who have said, With our tongue will we prevail; our lips are our own: who is lord over us?**

**12:5 For the oppression of the poor, for the sighing of the needy, now will I arise, saith the LORD; I will set him in safety from him that puffeth at him.**

**12:6 The words of the LORD are pure words: as silver tried in a furnace of earth, purified seven times.**

**12:7 Thou shalt keep them, O LORD, thou shalt preserve them from this generation for ever.**

**12:8 The wicked walk on every side, when the vilest men are exalted.**

## Psalm 13          11Q7

Psalm 13:1 How long wilt thou forget me, O LORD? For ever?
How long wilt thou hide thy face from me?
13:2 How long shall I take counsel in my soul, having sorrow in
my heart daily? How long shall mine enemy be exalted over me?
13:3 Consider and hear me, O LORD my God: lighten mine
eyes, lest I sleep the sleep of death;
13:4 Lest mine enemy say, I have prevailed against him; and
those that trouble me rejoice when I am moved.
13:5 But I have trusted in thy mercy; my heart shall rejoice in
thy salvation.
13:6 I will sing unto the LORD, because he hath dealt
bountifully with me.

## Psalm 14          11Q7

Psalm 14:1 The fool hath said in his heart, There is no God.
They are corrupt, they have done abominable works, there is
none that doeth good.
14:2 The LORD looked down from heaven upon the children of
men, to see if there were any that did understand, and seek God.
14:3 They are all gone aside, they are all together become filthy:
there is none that doeth good, no, not one.
14:4 Have all the workers of iniquity no knowledge? Who eat up
my people as they eat bread, and call not upon the LORD.
14:5 There were they in great fear: for God is in the generation
of the righteous.
14:6 Ye have shamed the counsel of the poor, because the LORD
is his refuge.
14:7 Oh that the salvation of Israel were come out of Zion! When
the LORD bringeth back the captivity of his people, Jacob shall
rejoice, and Israel shall be glad.

## Psalm 16     4Q85

**Psalm 16:1** Preserve me, O God: for in thee do I put my trust.
**16:2** O my soul, thou hast said unto the LORD, Thou art my Lord: my goodness extendeth not to thee;
**16:3** But to the saints that are in the earth, and to the excellent, in whom is all my delight.
**16:4** Their sorrows shall be multiplied that hasten after another god: their drink offerings of blood will I not offer, nor take up their names into my lips.
**16:5** The LORD is the portion of mine inheritance and of my cup: thou maintainest my lot.
**16:6 The lines are fallen unto me in pleasant places; yea, I have a goodly heritage.**
**16:7 I will bless the LORD, who hath given me counsel: my flesh also instruct me in the night seasons.**
**16:8 I have set the LORD always before me: because he is at my right hand, I shall not be moved.**
**16:9** Therefore my heart is glad, and my glory rejoiceth: my flesh also shall rest in hope.
**16:10** For thou wilt not leave my soul in hell; neither wilt thou suffer thine Holy One to see corruption.
**16:11** Thou wilt show me the path of life: in thy presence is fulness of joy; at thy right hand there are pleasures for evermore.

## Psalm 17          11Q7

**Psalm 17:1** Hear the right, O LORD, attend unto my cry, give ear unto my prayer, that goeth not out of feigned lips.

**17:2** Let my sentence come forth from thy presence; let thine eyes behold the things that are equal.

**17:3** Thou hast proved mine heart; thou hast visited me in the night; thou hast tried me, and shalt find nothing; I am purposed that my mouth shall not transgress.

**17:4** Concerning the works of men, by the word of thy lips I have kept me from the paths of the destroyer.

**17:5** Hold up my goings in thy paths, that my footsteps slip not.

**17:6** I have called upon thee, for thou wilt hear me, O God: incline thine ear unto me, and hear my speech.

**17:7** Show thy marvellous lovingkindness, O thou that savest by thy right hand them which put their trust in thee from those that rise up against them.

**17:8** Keep me as the apple of the eye, hide me under the shadow of thy wings,

**17:9 From the wicked that oppress me, from my deadly enemies, who compass me about.**

**17:10 They are inclosed in their own fat: with their mouth they speak proudly.**

**17:11 They have now compassed us in our steps: they have set their eyes bowing down to the earth;**

**17:12 Like as a lion that is greedy of his prey, and as it were a young lion lurking in secret places.**

**17:13 Arise, O LORD, disappoint him, cast him down: deliver my soul from the wicked, which is thy sword:**

**17:14 From men which are thy hand, O LORD, from men of the world, which have their portion in this life, and whose belly thou fillest with thy hid treasure: they are full of children, and leave the rest of their substance to their babes.**

**17:15 As for me, I will behold thy face in righteousness: I shall be satisfied, when I awake, with thy likeness.**

## Psalm 18        11Q7 & 11Q8 & 4Q85

Psalm 18:1    I will love thee, O LORD, my strength.

18:2 The LORD is my rock, and my fortress, and my deliverer; my God, my strength, in whom I will trust; my buckler, and the horn of my salvation, and my high tower.

18:3    I will call upon the LORD, who is worthy to be praised: so shall I be saved from mine enemies.

18:4 The sorrows of death compassed me, and the floods of ungodly men made me afraid.

18:5 The sorrows of hell compassed me about: the snares of death encompassed me.

18:6 In my distress I called upon the LORD, and cried unto my God: he heard my voice out of his temple, and my cry came before him, even into his ears.

18:7 Then the earth shook and trembled; the foundations also of the hills moved and were shaken, because he was wroth.

18:8 There went up a smoke out of his nostrils, and fire out of his mouth devoured: coals were kindled by it.

18:9 He bowed the heavens also, and came down: and darkness was under his feet.

18:10 And he rode upon a cherub, and did fly: yea, he did fly upon the wings of the wind.

18:11 He made darkness his secret place; his pavilion round about him were dark waters and thick clouds of the skies.

18:12 At the brightness that was before him his thick clouds passed, hail stones and coals of fire.

18:13 The LORD also thundered in the heavens, and the Highest gave his voice; hail stones and coals of fire.

18:14 Yea, he sent out his arrows, and scattered them; and he shot out lightnings, and discomfited them.

18:15 Then the channels of waters were seen, and the foundations of the world were discovered at thy rebuke, O LORD, at the blast of the breath of thy nostrils.

18:16 He sent from above, he took me, he drew me out of many waters.

**18:17** He delivered me from my strong enemy, and from them which hated me: for they were too strong for me.
**18:18** They encompassed me in the day of my calamity: but the LORD was my stay.
**18:19** He brought me forth also into a large place; he delivered me, because he delighted in me.
**18:20** The LORD rewarded me according to my righteousness; according to the cleanness of my hands hath he recompensed me.
**18:21** For I have kept the ways of the LORD, and have not wickedly departed from my God.
**18:22** For all his judgments were before me, and I did not put away his statutes from me.
**18:23** I was also upright before him, and I kept myself from mine iniquity.
**18:24** Therefore hath the LORD recompensed me according to my righteousness, according to the cleanness of my hands in his eyesight.
**18:25 With the merciful thou wilt show thyself merciful; with an upright man thou wilt show thyself upright;**
**18:26 With the pure thou wilt show thyself pure; and with the froward thou wilt show thyself froward.**
**18:27 For thou wilt save the afflicted people; but wilt bring down high looks.**
**18:28 For thou wilt light my candle: the LORD my God will enlighten my darkness.**
**18:29** For by thee I have run through a troop; and by my God have I leaped over a wall.
**18:30** As for God, his way is perfect: the word of the LORD is tried: he is a buckler to all those that trust in him.
**18:31 For who is God except the LORD? Or who is a rock except our God?**
**18:32 It is God that girdeth me with strength, and maketh my way perfect.**
**18:33 He maketh my feet like hinds' feet, and setteth me upon my high places.**
**18:34 He teacheth my hands to war, so that a bow of steel is bent**

by mine arms.

**18:35 Thou hast also given me the shield of thy salvation: and thy right hand hath holden me up, and thy gentleness hath made me great.**

**18:36** Thou hast enlarged my steps under me, that my feet did not slip.

**18:37** I have pursued mine enemies, and overtaken them: neither did I turn again till they were consumed.

**18:38 I have wounded them that they were not able to rise: they are fallen under my feet.**

**18:39 For thou hast girded me with strength unto the battle: thou hast subdued under me those that rose up against me.**

**18:40 Thou hast also given me the necks of mine enemies; that I might destroy them that hate me.**

**18:41 They cried, but there was none to save them: even unto the LORD, but he answered them not.**

**18:42** Then did I beat them small as the dust before the wind: I did cast them out as the dirt in the streets.

**18:43** Thou hast delivered me from the strivings of the people; and thou hast made me the head of the nations: a people whom I have not known shall serve me.

**18:44** As soon as they hear of me, they shall obey me: the strangers shall submit themselves unto me.

**18:45** The strangers shall fade away, and be afraid out of their closed places.

**18:46** The LORD liveth; and blessed be my rock; and let the God of my salvation be exalted.

**18:47** It is God that avengeth me, and subdueth the people under me.

**18:48** He delivereth me from mine enemies: yea, thou liftest me up above those that rise up against me: thou hast delivered me from the violent man.

**18:49** Therefore will I give thanks unto thee, O LORD, among the nations, and sing praises unto thy name.

**18:50** Great deliverance giveth he to his king; and showeth mercy to his anointed, to David, and to his descendants for evermore.

**Psalm 19**          **11Q7**

**Psalm 19:1** The heavens declare the glory of God; and the firmament showeth his handywork.

**19:2** Day unto day uttereth speech, and night unto night showeth knowledge.

**19:3 There is no speech nor language, where their voice is not heard.**

**19:4 Their line is gone out through all the earth, and their words to the end of the world. In them hath he set a tabernacle for the sun,**

**19:5 Which is as a bridegroom coming out of his chamber, and rejoiceth as a strong man to run a race.**

**19:6 His going forth is from the end of the heaven, and his circuit unto the ends of it: and there is nothing hid from the heat thereof.**

**19:7 The law of the LORD is perfect, converting the soul: the testimony of the LORD is sure, making wise the simple.**

**19:8** The statutes of the LORD are right, rejoicing the heart: the commandment of the LORD is pure, enlightening the eyes.

**19:9** The fear of the LORD is clean, enduring for ever: the judgments of the LORD are true and righteous altogether.

**19:10** More to be desired are they than gold, yea, than much fine gold: sweeter also than honey and the honeycomb.

**19:11** Moreover by them is thy servant warned: and in keeping of them there is great reward.

**19:12** Who can understand his errors? Cleanse thou me from secret faults.

**19:13** Keep back thy servant also from presumptuous sins; let them not have dominion over me: then shall I be upright, and I shall be innocent from the great transgression.

**19:14** Let the words of my mouth, and the meditation of my heart, be acceptable in thy sight, O LORD, my strength, and my redeemer.

**Psalm 22**　　　　　**4Q88**

**Psalm 22:1** My God, my God, why hast thou forsaken me? Why art thou so far from helping me, and from the words of my roaring?
**22:2** O my God, I cry in the day time, but thou hearest not; and in the night season, and am not silent.
**22:3** But thou art holy, O thou that inhabitest the praises of Israel.
**22:4** Our fathers trusted in thee: they trusted, and thou didst deliver them.
**22:5** They cried unto thee, and were delivered: they trusted in thee, and were not confounded.
**22:6** But I am a worm, and no man; a reproach of men, and despised of the people.
**22:7** All they that see me laugh me to scorn: they shoot out the lip, they shake the head, saying,
**22:8** He trusted on the LORD that he would deliver him: let him deliver him, seeing he delighted in him.
**22:9** But thou art he that took me out of the womb: thou didst make me hope when I was upon my mother's breasts.
**22:10** I was cast upon thee from the womb: thou art my God from my mother's belly.
**22:11** Be not far from me; for trouble is near; for there is none to help.
**22:12** Many bulls have compassed me: strong bulls of Bashan have beset me round.
**22:13** They gaped upon me with their mouths, as a ravening and a roaring lion.
**22:14 I am poured out like water, and all my bones are out of joint: my heart is like wax; it is melted in the midst of my bowels.**
**22:15 My strength is dried up like a potsherd; and my tongue cleaveth to my jaws; and thou hast brought me into the dust of death.**
**22:16 For dogs have compassed me: the assembly of the wicked have inclosed me: they pierced my hands and my feet.**
**22:17** I may tell all my bones: they look and stare upon me.

**22:18** They part my garments among them, and cast lots upon my vesture.
**22:19** But be not thou far from me, O LORD: O my strength, haste thee to help me.
**22:20** Deliver my soul from the sword; my darling from the power of the dog.
**22:21** Save me from the lion's mouth: for thou hast heard me from the horns of the unicorns.
**22:22** I will declare thy name unto my brethren: in the midst of the congregation will I praise thee.
**22:23** Ye that fear the LORD, praise him; all ye the seed of Jacob, glorify him; and fear him, all ye the seed of Israel.
**22:24** For he hath not despised nor abhorred the affliction of the afflicted; neither hath he hid his face from him; but when he cried unto him, he heard.
**22:25** My praise shall be of thee in the great congregation: I will pay my vows before them that fear him.
**22:26** The meek shall eat and be satisfied: they shall praise the LORD that seek him: your heart shall live for ever.
**22:27** All the ends of the world shall remember and turn unto the LORD: and all the kindreds of the nations shall worship before thee.
**22:28** For the kingdom is the LORD's: and he is the governor among the nations.
**22:29** All they that be fat upon earth shall eat and worship: all they that go down to the dust shall bow before him: and none can keep alive his own soul.
**22:30** A descendant shall serve him; it shall be accounted to the Lord for a generation.
**22:31** They shall come, and shall declare his righteousness unto a people that shall be born, that he hath done this.

## Psalm 25        11Q7 & 4Q83

**Psalm 25:1** Unto thee, O LORD, do I lift up my soul.
**25:2 O my God, I trust in thee: let me not be ashamed, let not mine enemies triumph over me.**
**25:3 Yea, let none that wait on thee be ashamed: let them be ashamed which transgress without cause.**
**25:4 Show me thy ways, O LORD; teach me thy paths.**
**25:5 Lead me in thy truth, and teach me: for thou art the God of my salvation; on thee do I wait all the day.**
**25:6 Remember, O LORD, thy tender mercies and thy lovingkindnesses; for they have been ever of old.**
**25:7 Remember not the sins of my youth, nor my transgressions: according to thy mercy remember thou me for thy goodness' sake, O LORD.**
**25:8 Good and upright is the LORD: therefore will he teach sinners in the way.**
**25:9 The meek will he guide in judgment: and the meek will he teach his way.**
**25:10 All the paths of the LORD are mercy and truth unto such as keep his covenant and his testimonies.**
**25:11 For thy name's sake, O LORD, pardon mine iniquity; for it is great.**
**25:12 What man is he that feareth the LORD? Him shall he teach in the way that he shall choose.**
**25:13** His soul shall dwell at ease; and his descendants shall inherit the earth.
**25:14** The secret of the LORD is with them that fear him; and he will show them his covenant.
**25:15 Mine eyes are ever toward the LORD; for he shall pluck my feet out of the net.**
**25:16** Turn thee unto me, and have mercy upon me; for I am desolate and afflicted.
**25:17** The troubles of my heart are enlarged: O bring thou me out of my distresses.
**25:18** Look upon mine affliction and my pain; and forgive all my

sins.

**25:19** Consider mine enemies; for they are many; and they hate me with cruel hatred.

**25:20** O keep my soul, and deliver me: let me not be ashamed; for I put my trust in thee.

**25:21** Let integrity and uprightness preserve me; for I wait on thee.

**25:22** Redeem Israel, O God, out of all his troubles.

## Psalm 26          4Q98(d)

**Psalm 26:1** Judge me, O LORD; for I have walked in mine integrity: I have trusted also in the LORD; therefore I shall not slide.
**26:2** Examine me, O LORD, and prove me; try my flesh and my heart.
**26:3** For thy lovingkindness is before mine eyes: and I have walked in thy truth.
**26:4** I have not sat with vain persons, neither will I go in with dissemblers.
**26:5** I have hated the congregation of evil doers; and will not be seated with the wicked.
**26:6** I will wash mine hands in innocency: so will I compass thine altar, O LORD:
**26:7 That I may publish with the voice of thanksgiving, and tell of all thy wondrous works.**
**26:8 LORD, I have loved the habitation of thy house, and the place where thine honour dwelleth.**
**26:9 Gather not my soul with sinners, nor my life with bloody men:**
**26:10 In whose hands is mischief, and their right hand is full of bribes.**
**26:11 But as for me, I will walk in mine integrity: redeem me, and be merciful unto me.**
**26:12 My foot standeth in an even place: in the congregations will I bless the LORD.**

## Psalm 27         4Q85

**Psalm 27:1** The LORD is my light and my salvation; whom shall I fear? The LORD is the strength of my life; of whom shall I be afraid?

**27:2** When the wicked, even mine enemies and my foes, came upon me to eat up my flesh, they stumbled and fell.

**27:3** Though an army should encamp against me, my heart shall not fear: though war should rise against me, in this will I be confident.

**27:4** One thing have I desired of the LORD, that will I seek after; that I may dwell in the house of the LORD all the days of my life, to behold the beauty of the LORD, and to enquire in his temple.

**27:5** For in the time of trouble he shall hide me in his pavilion: in the secret of his tabernacle shall he hide me; he shall set me up upon a rock.

**27:6** And now shall mine head be lifted up above mine enemies round about me: therefore will I offer in his tabernacle sacrifices of joy; I will sing, yea, I will sing praises unto the LORD.

**27:7** Hear, O LORD, when I cry with my voice: have mercy also upon me, and answer me.

**27:8** When thou saidst, Seek ye my face; my heart said unto thee, Thy face, LORD, will I seek.

**27:9** Hide not thy face far from me; put not thy servant away in anger: thou hast been my help; leave me not, neither forsake me, O God of my salvation.

**27:10** When my father and my mother forsake me, then the LORD will take me up.

**27:11** Teach me thy way, O LORD, and lead me in a plain path, because of mine enemies.

**27:12 Deliver me not over unto the will of mine enemies: for false witnesses are risen up against me, and such as breathe out cruelty.**

**27:13 I had fainted, unless I had believed to see the goodness of the LORD in the land of the living.**

**27:14 Wait on the LORD: be of good courage, and he shall strengthen thine heart: wait, I say, on the LORD.**

**Psalm 28**　　　　　**4Q85**

**Psalm 28:1 Unto thee will I cry, O LORD my rock; be not silent to me: lest, if thou be silent to me, I become like them that go down into the pit.**
**28:2 Hear the voice of my supplications, when I cry unto thee, when I lift up my hands toward thy holy oracle.**
**28:3 Draw me not away with the wicked, and with the workers of iniquity, which speak peace to their neighbours, but mischief is in their hearts.**
**28:4 Give them according to their deeds, and according to the wickedness of their endeavours: give them after the work of their hands; render to them their retribution.**
28:5 Because they regard not the works of the LORD, nor the operation of his hands, he shall destroy them, and not build them up.
**28:6** Blessed be the LORD, because he hath heard the voice of my supplications.
**28:7** The LORD is my strength and my shield; my heart trusted in him, and I am helped: therefore my heart greatly rejoiceth; and with my song will I praise him.
**28:8** The LORD is their strength, and he is the saving strength of his anointed.
**28:9** Save thy people, and bless thine inheritance: feed them also, and lift them up for ever.

## Psalm 30              4Q98(a)

**Psalm 30:1** I will extol thee, O LORD; for thou hast lifted me up, and hast not made my foes to rejoice over me.
**30:2** O LORD my God, I cried unto thee, and thou hast healed me.
**30:3** O LORD, thou hast brought up my soul from the grave: thou hast kept me alive, that I should not go down to the pit.
**30:4** Sing unto the LORD, O ye saints of his, and give thanks at the remembrance of his holiness.
**30:5** For his anger endureth but a moment; in his favour is life: weeping may endure for a night, but joy cometh in the morning.
**30:6** And in my prosperity I said, I shall never be moved.
**30:7** LORD, by thy favour thou hast made my mountain to stand strong: thou didst hide thy face, and I was troubled.
**30:8 I cried to thee, O LORD; and unto the LORD I made supplication.**
**30:9 What profit is there in my blood, when I go down to the pit? Shall the dust praise thee? Shall it declare thy truth?**
**30:10 Hear, O LORD, and have mercy upon me: LORD, be thou my helper.**
**30:11 Thou hast turned for me my mourning into dancing: thou hast put off my sackcloth, and girded me with gladness;**
**30:12 To the end that my glory may sing praise to thee, and not be silent.**
**O LORD my God, I will give thanks unto thee for ever.**

## Psalm 31          4Q83

**Psalm 31:1** In thee, O LORD, do I put my trust; let me never be ashamed: deliver me in thy righteousness.

**31:2** Bow down thine ear to me; deliver me speedily: be thou my strong rock, for an house of defense to save me.

**31:3** For thou art my rock and my fortress; therefore for thy name's sake lead me, and guide me.

**31:4** Pull me out of the net that they have laid privily for me: for thou art my strength.

**31:5** Into thine hand I commit my spirit: thou hast redeemed me, O LORD God of truth.

**31:6** I have hated them that regard lying vanities: but I trust in the LORD.

**31:7** I will be glad and rejoice in thy mercy: for thou hast considered my trouble; thou hast known my soul in adversities;

**31:8** And hast not shut me up into the hand of the enemy: thou hast set my feet in a large place.

**31:9** Have mercy upon me, O LORD, for I am in trouble: mine eye is consumed with grief, yea, my soul and my belly.

**31:10** For my life is spent with grief, and my years with sighing: my strength faileth because of mine iniquity, and my bones are consumed.

**31:11** I was a reproach among all mine enemies, but especially among my neighbours, and a fear to mine acquaintance: they that did see me without fled from me.

**31:12** I am forgotten as a dead man out of mind: I am like a broken vessel.

**31:13** For I have heard the slander of many: fear was on every side: while they took counsel together against me, they devised to take away my life.

**31:14** But I trusted in thee, O LORD: I said, Thou art my God.

**31:15** My times are in thy hand: deliver me from the hand of mine enemies, and from them that persecute me.

**31:16** Make thy face to shine upon thy servant: save me for thy mercies' sake.

**31:17** Let me not be ashamed, O LORD; for I have called upon thee: let the wicked be ashamed, and let them be silent in the grave.
**31:18** Let the lying lips be put to silence; which speak grievous things proudly and contemptuously against the righteous.
**31:19** Oh how great is thy goodness, which thou hast laid up for them that fear thee; which thou hast wrought for them that trust in thee before the sons of men!
**31:20** Thou shalt hide them in the secret of thy presence from the pride of man: thou shalt keep them secretly in a pavilion from the strife of tongues.
**31:21** Blessed be the LORD: for he hath showed me his marvellous kindness in a strong city.
**31:22 For I said in my haste, I am cut off from before thine eyes: nevertheless thou heardest the voice of my supplications when I cried unto thee.**
**31:23 O love the LORD, all ye his saints: for the LORD preserveth the faithful, and plentifully rewardeth the proud doer.**
**31:24 Be of good courage, and he shall strengthen your heart, all ye that hope in the LORD.**

## Psalm 33          4Q83 & 4Q98

Psalm 33:1 Rejoice in the LORD, O ye righteous: for praise is comely for the upright.

33:2 Praise the LORD with harp: sing unto him with the psaltery and an instrument of ten strings.

33:3 Sing unto him a new song; play skilfully with a loud noise.

33:4 For the word of the LORD is right; and all his works are done in truth.

33:5 He loveth righteousness and judgment: the earth is full of the goodness of the LORD.

33:6 By the word of the LORD were the heavens made; and all the army of them by the breath of his mouth.

33:7 He gathereth the waters of the sea together as an heap: he layeth up the depth in storehouses.

33:8 Let all the earth fear the LORD: let all the inhabitants of the world stand in awe of him.

33:9 For he spoke, and it was done; he commanded, and it stood fast.

33:10 The LORD bringeth the counsel of the nations to nought: he maketh the devices of the people of none effect.

33:11 The counsel of the LORD standeth for ever, the thoughts of his heart to all generations.

33:12 Blessed is the nation whose God is the LORD; and the people whom he hath chosen for his own inheritance.

33:13 The LORD looketh from heaven; he beholdeth all the sons of men.

33:14 From the place of his habitation he looketh upon all the inhabitants of the earth.

33:15 He fashioneth their hearts alike; he considereth all their works.

33:16 There is no king saved by the multitude of an army: a mighty man is not delivered by much strength.

33:17 An horse is a vain thing for safety: neither shall he deliver any by his great strength.

33:18 Behold, the eye of the LORD is upon them that fear him,

**upon them that hope in his mercy;**
**33:19** To deliver their soul from death, and to keep them alive in famine.
**33:20** Our soul waiteth for the LORD: he is our help and our shield.
**33:21** For our heart shall rejoice in him, because we have trusted in his holy name.
**33:22** Let thy mercy, O LORD, be upon us, according as we hope in thee.

## Psalm 34                4Q83

**Psalm 34:1** I will bless the LORD at all times: his praise shall continually be in my mouth.

**34:2** My soul shall make her boast in the LORD: the humble shall hear thereof, and be glad.

**34:3** O magnify the LORD with me, and let us exalt his name together.

**34:4** I sought the LORD, and he heard me, and delivered me from all my fears.

**34:5** They looked unto him, and were lightened: and their faces were not ashamed.

**34:6** This poor man cried, and the LORD heard him, and saved him out of all his troubles.

**34:7** The angel of the LORD encampeth round about them that fear him, and delivereth them.

**34:8** O taste and see that the LORD is good: blessed is the man that trusteth in him.

**34:9** O fear the LORD, ye his saints: for there is no want to them that fear him.

**34:10** The young lions do lack, and suffer hunger: but they that seek the LORD shall not want any good thing.

**34:11** Come, ye children, hearken unto me: I will teach you the fear of the LORD.

**34:12** What man is he that desireth life, and loveth many days, that he may see good?

**34:13** Keep thy tongue from evil, and thy lips from speaking guile.

**34:14** Depart from evil, and do good; seek peace, and pursue it.

**34:15** The eyes of the LORD are upon the righteous, and his ears are open unto their cry.

**34:16** The face of the LORD is against them that do evil, to cut off the remembrance of them from the earth.

**34:17** The righteous cry, and the LORD heareth, and delivereth them out of all their troubles.

**34:18** The LORD is nigh unto them that are of a broken heart; and saveth such as be of a contrite spirit.

**34:19** Many are the afflictions of the righteous: but the LORD delivereth him out of them all.
**34:20 He keepeth all his bones: not one of them is broken.**
**34:21 Evil shall slay the wicked: and they that hate the righteous shall be desolate.**
**34:22 The LORD redeemeth the soul of his servants: and none of them that trust in him shall be desolate.**

**Psalm 35**          **4Q83**

**Psalm 35:1** Plead my cause, O LORD, with them that strive with me: fight against them that fight against me.
**35:2** Take hold of shield and buckler, and stand up for mine help.
**35:3** Draw out also the spear, and stop the way against them that persecute me: say unto my soul, I am thy salvation.
**35:4** Let them be confounded and put to shame that seek after my soul: let them be turned back and brought to confusion that devise my hurt.
**35:5** Let them be as chaff before the wind: and let the angel of the LORD chase them.
**35:6** Let their way be dark and slippery: and let the angel of the LORD persecute them.
**35:7** For without cause have they hid for me their net in a pit, which without cause they have digged for my soul.
**35:8** Let destruction come upon him at unawares; and let his net that he hath hid catch himself: into that very destruction let him fall.
**35:9** And my soul shall be joyful in the LORD: it shall rejoice in his salvation.
**35:10** All my bones shall say, LORD, who is like unto thee, which deliverest the poor from him that is too strong for him, yea, the poor and the needy from him that plunders from him?
**35:11** False witnesses did rise up; they laid to my charge things that I knew not.
**35:12** They rewarded me evil for good to the plundering of my soul.
**35:13 But as for me, when they were sick, my clothing was sackcloth: I humbled my soul with fasting; and my prayer returned into mine own bosom.**
**35:14 I behaved myself as though he had been my friend or brother: I bowed down heavily, as one that mourneth for his mother.**
**35:15 But in mine adversity they rejoiced, and gathered themselves together: yea, the smiters gathered themselves together against me, and I knew it not; they did tear me, and ceased not:**

35:16 With hypocritical mockers in feasts, they gnashed upon me with their teeth.
35:17 Lord, how long wilt thou look on? Rescue my soul from their destructions, my darling from the lions.
35:18 I will give thee thanks in the great congregation: I will praise thee among much people.
35:19 Let not them that are mine enemies wrongfully rejoice over me: neither let them wink with the eye that hate me without a cause.
35:20 For they speak not peace: but they devise deceitful matters against them that are quiet in the land.
35:21 Yea, they opened their mouth wide against me, and said, Aha, aha, our eye hath seen it.
35:22 This thou hast seen, O LORD: keep not silence: O Lord, be not far from me.
35:23 Stir up thyself, and awake to my judgment, even unto my cause, my God and my Lord.
35:24 Judge me, O LORD my God, according to thy righteousness; and let them not rejoice over me.
35:25 Let them not say in their hearts, Ah, so would we have it: let them not say, We have swallowed him up.
35:26 Let them be ashamed and brought to confusion together that rejoice at mine hurt: let them be clothed with shame and dishonour that magnify themselves against me.
35:27 Let them shout for joy, and be glad, that favour my righteous cause: yea, let them say continually, Let the LORD be magnified, which hath pleasure in the prosperity of his servant.
35:28 And my tongue shall speak of thy righteousness and of thy praise all the day long.

## Psalm 36                    4Q83 & 11Q8

Psalm 36:1 The transgression of the wicked saith within my heart, that there is no fear of God before his eyes.

36:2 For he flattereth himself in his own eyes, until his iniquity be found to be hateful.

36:3 The words of his mouth are iniquity and deceit: he hath left off to be wise, and to do good.

36:4 He deviseth mischief upon his bed; he setteth himself in a way that is not good; he abhorreth not evil.

36:5 Thy mercy, O LORD, is in the heavens; and thy faithfulness reacheth unto the clouds.

36:6 Thy righteousness is like the great mountains; thy judgments are a great deep: O LORD, thou preservest man and beast.

36:7 How excellent is thy lovingkindness, O God! Therefore the children of men put their trust under the shadow of thy wings.

36:8 They shall be fully satisfied with the abundance of thy house; and thou shalt make them drink of the river of thy pleasures.

36:9 For with thee is the fountain of life: in thy light shall we see light.

36:10 O continue thy lovingkindness unto them that know thee; and thy righteousness to the upright in heart.

36:11 Let not the foot of pride come against me, and let not the hand of the wicked remove me.

36:12 There are the workers of iniquity fallen: they are cast down, and shall not be able to rise.

## Psalm 37  11Q8 & 4Q85

**Psalm 37:1 Fret not thyself because of evildoers, neither be thou envious against the workers of iniquity.**
**37:2 For they shall soon be cut down like the grass, and wither as the green herb.**
**37:3 Trust in the LORD, and do good; so shalt thou dwell in the land, and verily thou shalt be fed.**
**37:4 Delight thyself also in the LORD: and he shall give thee the desires of thine heart.**
**37:5** Commit thy way unto the LORD; trust also in him; and he shall bring it to pass.
**37:6** And he shall bring forth thy righteousness as the light, and thy judgment as the noonday.
**37:7** Rest in the LORD, and wait patiently for him: fret not thyself because of him who prospereth in his way, because of the man who bringeth wicked devices to pass.
**37:8** Cease from anger, and forsake wrath: fret not thyself in any wise to do evil.
**37:9** For evildoers shall be cut off: but those that wait upon the LORD, they shall inherit the earth.
**37:10** For yet a little while, and the wicked shall not be: yea, thou shalt diligently consider his place, and it shall not be.
**37:11** But the meek shall inherit the earth; and shall delight themselves in the abundance of peace.
**37:12** The wicked plotteth against the just, and gnasheth upon him with his teeth.
**37:13** The LORD shall laugh at him: for he seeth that his day is coming.
**37:14** The wicked have drawn out the sword, and have bent their bow, to cast down the poor and needy, and to slay such as be of upright conversation.
**37:15** Their sword shall enter into their own heart, and their bows shall be broken.
**37:16** A little that a righteous man hath is better than the riches of many wicked.

**37:17** For the arms of the wicked shall be broken: but the LORD upholdeth the righteous.

**37:18 The LORD knoweth the days of the upright: and their inheritance shall be for ever.**

**37:19 They shall not be ashamed in the evil time: and in the days of famine they shall be satisfied.**

**37:20** But the wicked shall perish, and the enemies of the LORD shall be as the fat of lambs: they shall consume; into smoke shall they consume away.

**37:21** The wicked borroweth, and payeth not again: but the righteous showeth mercy, and giveth.

**37:22** For such as be blessed of him shall inherit the earth; and they that be cursed of him shall be cut off.

**37:23** The steps of a good man are ordered by the LORD: and he delighteth in his way.

**37:24** Though he fall, he shall not be utterly cast down: for the LORD upholdeth him with his hand.

**37:25** I have been young, and now am old; yet have I not seen the righteous forsaken, nor his descendants begging bread.

**37:26** He is ever merciful, and lendeth; and his descendants are blessed.

**37:27** Depart from evil, and do good; and dwell for evermore.

**37:28** For the LORD loveth judgment, and forsaketh not his saints; they are preserved for ever: but the descendants of the wicked shall be cut off.

**37:29** The righteous shall inherit the land, and dwell therein for ever.

**37:30** The mouth of the righteous speaketh wisdom, and his tongue talketh of judgment.

**37:31** The law of his God is in his heart; none of his steps shall slide.

**37:32** The wicked watcheth the righteous, and seeketh to slay him.

**37:33** The LORD will not leave him in his hand, nor condemn him when he is judged.

**37:34** Wait on the LORD, and keep his way, and he shall exalt thee to inherit the land: when the wicked are cut off, thou shalt see it.

**37:35** I have seen the wicked in great power, and spreading himself like a green bay tree.

**37:36** Yet he passed away, and, lo, he was not: yea, I sought him, but he could not be found.

**37:37** Mark the perfect man, and behold the upright: for the end of that man is peace.

**37:38** But the transgressors shall be destroyed together: the end of the wicked shall be cut off.

**37:39** But the salvation of the righteous is of the LORD: he is their strength in the time of trouble.

**37:40** And the LORD shall help them, and deliver them: he shall deliver them from the wicked, and save them, because they trust in him.

## Psalm 38          4Q83

**Psalm 38:1** O lord, rebuke me not in thy wrath: neither chasten me in thy hot displeasure.

**38:2** For thine arrows stick fast in me, and thy hand presseth me sore.

**38:3** There is no soundness in my flesh because of thine anger; neither is there any rest in my bones because of my sin.

**38:4** For mine iniquities are gone over mine head: as an heavy burden they are too heavy for me.

**38:5** My wounds stink and are corrupt because of my foolishness.

**38:6** I am troubled; I am bowed down greatly; I go mourning all the day long.

**38:7** For my loins are filled with a loathsome disease: and there is no soundness in my flesh.

**38:8** I am feeble and sore broken: I have roared by reason of the disquietness of my heart.

**38:9** Lord, all my desire is before thee; and my groaning is not hid from thee.

**38:10** My heart panteth, my strength faileth me: as for the light of mine eyes, it also is gone from me.

**38:11** My loved ones and my friends stand aloof from my sore; and my kinsmen stand afar off.

**38:12** They also that seek after my life lay snares for me: and they that seek my hurt speak mischievous things, and imagine deceits all the day long.

**38:13** But I, as a deaf man, heard not; and I was as a dumb man that openeth not his mouth.

**38:14** Thus I was as a man that heareth not, and in whose mouth are no reproofs.

**38:15 For in thee, O LORD, do I hope: thou wilt hear, O Lord my God.**

**38:16 For I said, Hear me, lest otherwise they should rejoice over me: when my foot slippeth, they magnify themselves against me.**

**38:17 For I am ready to halt, and my sorrow is continually**

before me.

38:18 For I will declare mine iniquity; I will be sorry for my sin.

38:19 But mine enemies are lively, and they are strong: and they that hate me wrongfully are multiplied.

38:20 They also that render evil for good are mine adversaries; because I follow the thing that good is.

38:21 Forsake me not, O LORD: O my God, be not far from me.

38:22 Make haste to help me, O Lord my salvation.

**Psalm 43**          **11Q8**

**Psalm 43:1 Judge me, O God, and plead my cause against an ungodly nation: O deliver me from the deceitful and unjust man. 43:2 For thou art the God of my strength: why dost thou cast me off? Why go I mourning because of the oppression of the enemy?**
**43:3 O send out thy light and thy truth: let them lead me; let them bring me unto thy holy hill, and to thy tabernacles.**
**43:4** Then will I go unto the altar of God, unto God my exceeding joy: yea, upon the harp will I praise thee, O God my God.
**43:5** Why art thou cast down, O my soul? And why art thou disquieted within me? Hope in God: for I shall yet praise him, who is the health of my countenance, and my God.

## Psalm 44          1Q12 & 4Q85

**Psalm 44:1** We have heard with our ears, O God, our fathers have told us, what work thou didst in their days, in the times of old.
**44:2 How thou didst drive out the nations with thy hand, and plantedst them; how thou didst afflict the people, and cast them out.**
**44:3 For they got not the land in possession by their own sword, neither did their own arm save them: but thy right hand, and thine arm, and the light of thy countenance, because thou hadst a favour unto them.**
**44:4 Thou art my King, O God: command deliverances for Jacob.**
**44:5** Through thee will we push down our enemies: through thy name will we tread them under that rise up against us.
**44:6 For I will not trust in my bow, neither shall my sword save me.**
**44:7 But thou hast saved us from our enemies, and hast put them to shame that hated us.**
**44:8 In God we boast all the day long, and praise thy name for ever.**
**Selah.**
**44:9** But thou hast cast off, and put us to shame; and goest not forth with our armies.
**44:10** Thou makest us to turn back from the enemy: and they which hate us steal for themselves.
**44:11** Thou hast given us like sheep appointed for meat; and hast scattered us among the heathen.
**44:12** Thou sellest thy people for nought, and dost not increase thy wealth by their price.
**44:13** Thou makest us a reproach to our neighbours, a scorn and a derision to them that are round about us.
**44:14** Thou makest us a byword among the nations, a shaking of the head among the people.
**44:15** My confusion is continually before me, and the shame of my face hath covered me,

45

**44:16** For the voice of him that reproacheth and blasphemeth; by reason of the enemy and avenger.

**44:17** All this is come upon us; yet have we not forgotten thee, neither have we dealt falsely in thy covenant.

**44:18** Our heart is not turned back, neither have our steps declined from thy way;

**44:19** Though thou hast sore broken us in the place of dragons, and covered us with the shadow of death.

**44:20** If we have forgotten the name of our God, or stretched out our hands to a strange god;

**44:21** Shall not God search this out? For he knoweth the secrets of the heart.

**44:22 Yea, for thy sake are we killed all the day long; we are counted as sheep for the slaughter.**

**44:23 Awake, why sleepest thou, O Lord? Arise, cast us not off for ever.**

**44:24 Wherefore hidest thou thy face, and forgettest our affliction and our oppression?**

**44:25** For our soul is bowed down to the dust: our belly cleaveth unto the earth.

**44:26** Arise for our help, and redeem us for thy mercies' sake.

## Psalm 48                4Q91

**Psalm 48:1 Great is the LORD, and greatly to be praised in the city of our God, in the mountain of his holiness.**
**48:2 Beautiful for situation, the joy of the whole earth, is mount Zion, on the sides of the north, the city of the great King.**
**48:3 God is known in her palaces for a refuge.**
**48:4 For, lo, the kings were assembled, they passed by together.**
**48:5 They saw it, and so they marvelled; they were troubled, and hasted away.**
**48:6 Fear took hold upon them there, and pain, as of a woman in travail.**
**48:7 Thou breakest the ships of Tarshish with an east wind.**
**48:8 As we have heard, so have we seen in the city of the LORD of armies, in the city of our God: God will establish it for ever. Selah.**
**48:9** We have thought of thy lovingkindness, O God, in the midst of thy temple.
**48:10** According to thy name, O God, so is thy praise unto the ends of the earth: thy right hand is full of righteousness.
**48:11** Let mount Zion rejoice, let the daughters of Judah be glad, because of thy judgments.
**48:12** Walk about Zion, and go round about her: tell the towers thereof.
**48:13** Mark ye well her bulwarks, consider her palaces; that ye may tell it to the generation following.
**48:14** For this God is our God for ever and ever: he will be our guide even unto death.

**Psalm 49**          **4Q85 & 4Q91**

Psalm 49:1 Hear this, all ye people; give ear, all ye inhabitants of the world:

49:2 Both low and high, rich and poor, together.

49:3 My mouth shall speak of wisdom; and the meditation of my heart shall be of understanding.

49:4 I will incline mine ear to a parable: I will open my dark saying upon the harp.

49:5 Wherefore should I fear in the days of evil, when the iniquity of my foes shall compass me about?

49:6 They that trust in their wealth, and boast themselves in the multitude of their riches;

49:7 None of them can by any means redeem his brother, nor give to God a ransom for him:

49:8 For the redemption of their soul is costly, and it ceaseth for ever:

49:9 That he should still live for ever, and not see corruption.

49:10 For he seeth that wise men die, likewise the fool and the brutish person perish, and leave their wealth to others.

49:11 Their inward thought is, that their houses shall continue for ever, and their dwelling places to all generations; they call their lands after their own names.

49:12 Nevertheless man being in honour abideth not: he is like the beasts that perish.

49:13 This their way is their folly: yet their posterity approve their sayings. Selah.

49:14 Like sheep they are laid in the grave; death shall feed on them; and the upright shall have dominion over them in the morning; and their beauty shall consume in the grave from their dwelling.

49:15 But God will redeem my soul from the power of the grave: for he shall receive me. Selah.

49:16 Be not thou afraid when one is made rich, when the glory of his house is increased;

49:17 For when he dieth he shall carry nothing away: his glory shall not descend after him.

**49:18** Though while he lived he blessed his soul: and men will praise thee, when thou doest well to thyself.

**49:19** He shall go to the generation of his fathers; they shall never see light.

**49:20** Man that is in honour, and understandeth not, is like the beasts that perish.

## Psalm 50          11Q9 & 4Q85

**Psalm 50:1** The mighty God, even the LORD, hath spoken, and called the earth from the rising of the sun unto the going down thereof.

**50:2** Out of Zion, the perfection of beauty, God hath shined.

**50:3 Our God shall come, and shall not keep silence: a fire shall devour before him, and it shall be very tempestuous round about him.**

**50:4 He shall call to the heavens from above, and to the earth, that he may judge his people.**

**50:5 Gather my saints together unto me; those that have made a covenant with me by sacrifice.**

**50:6 And the heavens shall declare his righteousness: for God is judge himself. Selah.**

**50:7 Hear, O my people, and I will speak; O Israel, and I will testify against thee: I am God, even thy God.**

**50:8** I will not reprove thee for thy sacrifices or thy burnt offerings, to have been continually before me.

**50:9** I will take no bullock out of thy house, nor he goats out of thy folds.

**50:10** For every beast of the forest is mine, and the cattle upon a thousand hills.

**50:11** I know all the fowls of the mountains: and the wild beasts of the field are mine.

**50:12** If I were hungry, I would not tell thee: for the world is mine, and the fulness thereof.

**50:13 Will I eat the flesh of bulls, or drink the blood of goats?**

**50:14 Offer unto God thanksgiving; and pay thy vows unto the most High:**

**50:15 And call upon me in the day of trouble: I will deliver thee, and thou shalt glorify me.**

**50:16 But unto the wicked God saith, What hast thou to do to declare my statutes, or that thou shouldest take my covenant in thy mouth?**

**50:17 Seeing thou hatest instruction, and casteth my words**

behind thee.

50:18 When thou sawest a thief, then thou consentedst with him, and hast been partaker with adulterers.

50:19 Thou givest thy mouth to evil, and thy tongue frameth deceit.

50:20 Thou are seated and speakest against thy brother; thou slanderest thine own mother's son.

50:21 These things hast thou done, and I kept silence; thou thoughtest that I was altogether such an one as thyself: but I will reprove thee, and set them in order before thine eyes.

50:22 Now consider this, ye that forget God, lest I tear you in pieces, and there be none to deliver.

50:23 Whoso offereth praise glorifieth me: and to him that ordereth his conversation aright will I show the salvation of God.

## Psalm 52        4Q85

**Psalm 52:1** Why boastest thou thyself in mischief, O mighty man? The goodness of God endureth continually.

**52:2** The tongue deviseth mischiefs; like a sharp razor, working deceitfully.

**52:3 Thou lovest evil more than good; and lying rather than to speak righteousness. Selah.**

**52:4 Thou lovest all devouring words, O thou deceitful tongue.**

**52:5 God shall likewise destroy thee for ever, he shall take thee away, and pluck thee out of thy dwelling place, and root thee out of the land of the living. Selah.**

**52:6 The righteous also shall see, and fear, and shall laugh at him:**

**52:7 Lo, this is the man that made not God his strength; but trusted in the abundance of his riches, and strengthened himself in his wickedness.**

**52:8 But I am like a green olive tree in the house of God: I trust in the mercy of God for ever and ever.**

**52:9 I will praise thee for ever, because thou hast done it: and I will wait on thy name; for it is good before thy saints.**

**Psalm 53**            **4Q83**

**Psalm 53:1 The fool hath said in his heart, There is no God. Corrupt are they, and have done abominable iniquity: there is none that doeth good.**
**53:2 God looked down from heaven upon the children of men, to see if there were any that did understand, that did seek God.**
**53:3 Every one of them is gone back: they are altogether become filthy; there is none that doeth good, no, not one.**
**53:4 Have the workers of iniquity no knowledge? Who eat up my people as they eat bread: they have not called upon God.**
**53:5 There were they in great fear, where no fear was: for God hath scattered the bones of him that encampeth against thee: thou hast put them to shame, because God hath despised them.**
**53:6 Oh that the salvation of Israel were come out of Zion! When God bringeth back the captivity of his people, Jacob shall rejoice, and Israel shall be glad.**

## Psalm 54                    4Q83

**Psalm 54:1 Save me, O God, by thy name, and judge me by thy strength.**
**54:2 Hear my prayer, O God; give ear to the words of my mouth.**
**54:3 For strangers are risen up against me, and oppressors seek after my soul: they have not set God before them. Selah.**
**54:4 Behold, God is mine helper: the Lord is with them that uphold my soul.**
**54:5** He shall reward evil unto mine enemies: cut them off in thy truth.
**54:6** I will freely sacrifice unto thee: I will praise thy name, O LORD; for it is good.
**54:7** For he hath delivered me out of all trouble: and mine eye hath seen his desire upon mine enemies.

**Psalm 59**            **11Q8**

**Psalm 59:1** Deliver me from mine enemies, O my God: defend me from them that rise up against me.
**59:2** Deliver me from the workers of iniquity, and save me from bloody men.
**59:3** For, lo, they lie in wait for my soul: the mighty are gathered against me; not for my transgression, nor for my sin, O LORD.
**59:4** They run and prepare themselves without my fault: awake to help me, and behold.
**59:5 Thou therefore, O LORD God of armies, the God of Israel, awake to visit all the nations: be not merciful to any wicked transgressors. Selah.**
**59:6 They return at evening: they make a noise like a dog, and go round about the city.**
**59:7 Behold, they belch out with their mouth: swords are in their lips: for who, say they, doth hear?**
**59:8 But thou, O LORD, shalt laugh at them; thou shalt have all the nations in derision.**
**59:9** Because of his strength will I wait upon thee: for God is my defense.
**59:10** The God of my mercy shall meet me: God shall let me see my desire upon mine enemies.
**59:11** Slay them not, lest my people forget: scatter them by thy power; and bring them down, O Lord our shield.
**59:12** For the sin of their mouth and the words of their lips let them even be taken in their pride: and for cursing and lying which they speak.
**59:13** Consume them in wrath, consume them, that they may not be: and let them know that God ruleth in Jacob unto the ends of the earth. Selah.
**59:14** And at evening let them return; and let them make a noise like a dog, and go round about the city.
**59:15** Let them wander up and down for meat, and growl if they be not satisfied.
**59:16** But I will sing of thy power; yea, I will sing aloud of thy

mercy in the morning: for thou hast been my defense and refuge in the day of my trouble.

**59:17** Unto thee, O my strength, will I sing: for God is my defense, and the God of my mercy.

## Psalm 66          4Q83

**Psalm 66:1** Make a joyful noise unto God, all ye lands:

**66:2** Sing forth the honour of his name: make his praise glorious.

**66:3** Say unto God, How terrible art thou in thy works! Through the greatness of thy power shall thine enemies submit themselves unto thee.

**66:4** All the earth shall worship thee, and shall sing unto thee; they shall sing to thy name. Selah.

**66:5** Come and see the works of God: he is terrible in his doing toward the children of men.

**66:6** He turned the sea into dry land: they went through the flood on foot: there did we rejoice in him.

**66:7** He ruleth by his power for ever; his eyes behold the nations: let not the rebellious exalt themselves. Selah.

**66:8** O bless our God, ye people, and make the voice of his praise to be heard:

**66:9** Which holdeth our soul in life, and suffereth not our feet to be moved.

**66:10** For thou, O God, hast proved us: thou hast tried us, as silver is tried.

**66:11** Thou broughtest us into the net; thou laidst affliction upon our loins.

**66:12** Thou hast caused men to ride over our heads; we went through fire and through water: but thou broughtest us out into a wealthy place.

**66:13** I will go into thy house with burnt offerings: I will pay thee my vows,

**66:14** Which my lips have uttered, and my mouth hath spoken, when I was in trouble.

**66:15** I will offer unto thee burnt sacrifices of fatlings, with the incense of rams; I will offer bullocks with goats. Selah.

**66:16 Come and hear, all ye that fear God, and I will declare what he hath done for my soul.**

**66:17 I cried unto him with my mouth, and he was extolled with my tongue.**

66:18 If I regard iniquity in my heart, the Lord will not hear me:

66:19 But verily God hath heard me; he hath attended to the voice of my prayer.

66:20 Blessed be God, which hath not turned away my prayer, nor his mercy from me.

Psalm 67                    4Q83

Psalm 67:1 God be merciful unto us, and bless us; and cause his face to shine upon us; Selah.

67:2 That thy way may be known upon earth, thy saving health among all nations.

67:3 Let the people praise thee, O God; let all the people praise thee.

67:4 O let the nations be glad and sing for joy: for thou shalt judge the people righteously, and govern the nations upon earth. Selah.

67:5 Let the people praise thee, O God; let all the people praise thee.

67:6 Then shall the earth yield her increase; and God, even our own God, shall bless us.

67:7 God shall bless us; and all the ends of the earth shall fear him.

**Psalm 68**              **11Q8**

**Psalm 68:1 Let God arise, let his enemies be scattered: let them also that hate him flee before him.**
**68:2 As smoke is driven away, so drive them away: as wax melteth before the fire, so let the wicked perish at the presence of God.**
**68:3 But let the righteous be glad; let them rejoice before God: yea, let them exceedingly rejoice.**
**68:4 Sing unto God, sing praises to his name: extol him that rideth upon the heavens by his name the LORD, and rejoice before him.**
**68:5** A father of the fatherless, and a judge of the widows, is God in his holy habitation.
**68:6** God setteth the solitary in families: he bringeth out those which are bound with chains: but the rebellious dwell in a dry land.
**68:7** O God, when thou wentest forth before thy people, when thou didst march through the wilderness; Selah:
**68:8** The earth shook, the heavens also dropped at the presence of God: even Sinai itself was moved at the presence of God, the God of Israel.
**68:9** Thou, O God, didst send a plentiful rain, whereby thou didst confirm thine inheritance, when it was weary.
**68:10** Thy congregation hath dwelt therein: thou, O God, hast prepared of thy goodness for the poor.
**68:11** The Lord gave the word: great was the company of those that published it.
**68:12** Kings of armies did flee apace: and she that tarried at home divided the plunder.
**68:13 Though ye have lien among the pots, yet shall ye be as the wings of a dove covered with silver, and her feathers with yellow gold.**
**68:14 When the Almighty scattered kings in it, it was white as snow in Salmon.**
**68:15 The hill of God is as the hill of Bashan; an high hill as the hill of Bashan.**

**68:16** Why leap ye, ye high hills? This is the hill which God desireth to dwell in; yea, the LORD will dwell in it for ever.
**68:17** The chariots of God are twenty thousand, even thousands of angels: the Lord is among them, as in Sinai, in the holy place.
**68:18** Thou hast ascended on high, thou hast led captivity captive: thou hast received gifts for men; yea, for the rebellious also, that the LORD God might dwell among them.
**68:19** Blessed be the Lord, who daily loadeth us with benefits, even the God of our salvation. Selah.
**68:20** He that is our God is the God of salvation; and unto GOD the Lord belong the issues from death.
**68:21** But God shall wound the head of his enemies, and the hairy scalp of such an one as goeth on still in his trespasses.
**68:22** The Lord said, I will bring again from Bashan, I will bring my people again from the depths of the sea:
**68:23** That thy foot may be dipped in the blood of thine enemies, and the tongue of thy dogs in the same.
**68:24** They have seen thy goings, O God; even the goings of my God, my King, in the sanctuary.
**68:25** The singers went before, the players on instruments followed after; among them were the damsels playing with timbrels.
**68:26** Bless ye God in the congregations, even the Lord, from the fountain of Israel.
**68:27** There is little Benjamin with their ruler, the princes of Judah and their council, the princes of Zebulun, and the princes of Naphtali.
**68:28** Thy God hath commanded thy strength: strengthen, O God, that which thou hast wrought for us.
**68:29** Because of thy temple at Jerusalem shall kings bring presents unto thee.
**68:30** Rebuke the company of spearmen, the multitude of the bulls, with the calves of the people, till every one submit himself with pieces of silver: scatter thou the people that delight in war.
**68:31** Princes shall come out of Egypt; Ethiopia shall soon stretch out her hands unto God.
**68:32** Sing unto God, ye kingdoms of the earth; O sing praises unto

the Lord; Selah:

**68:33** To him that rideth upon the heavens of heavens, which were of old; lo, he doth send out his voice, and that a mighty voice.

**68:34** Ascribe ye strength unto God: his excellency is over Israel, and his strength is in the clouds.

**68:35** O God, thou art terrible out of thy holy places: the God of Israel is he that giveth strength and power unto his people. Blessed be God.

Psalm 69          4Q83

Psalm 69:1 Save me, O God; for the waters are come in unto my soul.

69:2 I sink in deep mire, where there is no standing: I am come into deep waters, where the floods overflow me.

69:3 I am weary of my crying: my throat is dried: mine eyes fail while I wait for my God.

69:4 They that hate me without a cause are more than the hairs of mine head: they that would destroy me, being mine enemies wrongfully, are mighty: then I restored that which I took not away.

69:5 O God, thou knowest my foolishness; and my sins are not hid from thee.

69:6 Let not them that wait on thee, O Lord GOD of armies, be ashamed for my sake: let not those that seek thee be confounded for my sake, O God of Israel.

69:7 Because for thy sake I have borne reproach; shame hath covered my face.

69:8 I am become a stranger unto my brethren, and an alien unto my mother's children.

69:9 For the zeal of thine house hath eaten me up; and the reproaches of them that reproached thee are fallen upon me.

69:10 When I wept, and chastened my soul with fasting, that was to my reproach.

69:11 I made sackcloth also my garment; and I became a proverb to them.

69:12 They that are seated in the gate speak against me; and I was the song of the drunkards.

69:13 But as for me, my prayer is unto thee, O LORD, in an acceptable time: O God, in the multitude of thy mercy hear me, in the truth of thy salvation.

69:14 Deliver me out of the mire, and let me not sink: let me be delivered from them that hate me, and out of the deep waters.

69:15 Let not the flood waters overflow me, neither let the deep swallow me up, and let not the pit shut her mouth upon me.

**69:16 Hear me, O LORD; for thy lovingkindness is good: turn unto me according to the multitude of thy tender mercies.**
**69:17 And hide not thy face from thy servant; for I am in trouble: hear me speedily.**
**69:18 Draw nigh unto my soul, and redeem it: deliver me because of mine enemies.**
**69:19** Thou hast known my reproach, and my shame, and my dishonour: mine adversaries are all before thee.
**69:20** Reproach hath broken my heart; and I am full of heaviness: and I looked for some to take pity, but there was none; and for comforters, but I found none.
**69:21** They gave me also gall for my food; and in my thirst they gave me vinegar to drink.
**69:22** Let their table become a snare before them: and that which should have been for their welfare, let it become a trap.
**69:23** Let their eyes be darkened, that they see not; and make their loins continually to shake.
**69:24** Pour out thine indignation upon them, and let thy wrathful anger take hold of them.
**69:25** Let their habitation be desolate; and let none dwell in their tents.
**69:26** For they persecute him whom thou hast smitten; and they talk to the grief of those whom thou hast wounded.
**69:27** Add iniquity unto their iniquity: and let them not come into thy righteousness.
**69:28** Let them be blotted out of the book of the living, and not be written with the righteous.
**69:29** But I am poor and sorrowful: let thy salvation, O God, set me up on high.
**69:30** I will praise the name of God with a song, and will magnify him with thanksgiving.
**69:31** This also shall please the LORD better than an ox or bullock that hath horns and hoofs.
**69:32** The humble shall see this, and be glad: and your heart shall live that seek God.
**69:33** For the LORD heareth the poor, and despiseth not his

prisoners.

**69:34** Let the heaven and earth praise him, the seas, and every thing that moveth therein.

**69:35** For God will save Zion, and will build the cities of Judah: that they may dwell there, and have it in possession.

**69:36** The seed also of his servants shall inherit it: and they that love his name shall dwell therein.

## Psalm 71          4Q83

Psalm 71:1 In thee, O LORD, do I put my trust: let me never be put to confusion.

71:2 Deliver me in thy righteousness, and cause me to escape: incline thine ear unto me, and save me.

71:3 Be thou my strong habitation, whereunto I may continually resort: thou hast given commandment to save me; for thou art my rock and my fortress.

71:4 Deliver me, O my God, out of the hand of the wicked, out of the hand of the unrighteous and cruel man.

71:5 For thou art my hope, O Lord GOD: thou art my trust from my youth.

71:6 By thee have I been holden up from the womb: thou art he that took me out of my mother's belly: my praise shall be continually of thee.

71:7 I am as a wonder unto many; but thou art my strong refuge.

71:8 Let my mouth be filled with thy praise and with thy honour all the day.

71:9 Cast me not off in the time of old age; forsake me not when my strength faileth.

71:10 For mine enemies speak against me; and they that lay wait for my soul take counsel together,

71:11 Saying, God hath forsaken him: persecute and take him; for there is none to deliver him.

71:12 O God, be not far from me: O my God, make haste for my help.

71:13 Let them be confounded and consumed that are adversaries to my soul; let them be covered with reproach and dishonour that seek my hurt.

71:14 But I will hope continually, and will yet praise thee more and more.

71:15 My mouth shall show forth thy righteousness and thy salvation all the day; for I know not the numbers thereof.

71:16 I will go in the strength of the Lord GOD: I will make mention of thy righteousness, even of thine only.

**71:17** O God, thou hast taught me from my youth: and hitherto have I declared thy wondrous works.

**71:18** Now also when I am old and greyheaded, O God, forsake me not; until I have showed thy strength unto this generation, and thy power to every one that is to come.

**71:19** Thy righteousness also, O God, is very high, who hast done great things: O God, who is like unto thee!

**71:20** Thou, which hast showed me great and sore troubles, shalt quicken me again, and shalt bring me up again from the depths of the earth.

**71:21** Thou shalt increase my greatness, and comfort me on every side.

**71:22** I will also praise thee with the psaltery, even thy truth, O my God: unto thee will I sing with the harp, O thou Holy One of Israel.

**71:23** My lips shall greatly rejoice when I sing unto thee; and my soul, which thou hast redeemed.

**71:24** My tongue also shall talk of thy righteousness all the day long: for they are confounded, for they are brought unto shame, that seek my hurt.

**Psalm 76**          **4Q87**

**Psalm 76:1** In Judah is God known: his name is great in Israel.
**76:2** In Salem also is his tabernacle, and his dwelling place in Zion.
**76:3** There brake he the arrows of the bow, the shield, and the sword, and the battle. Selah.
**76:4** Thou art more glorious and excellent than the mountains of prey.
**76:5** The stouthearted are plundered, they have slept their sleep: and none of the men of might have found their hands.
**76:6** At thy rebuke, O God of Jacob, both the chariot and horse are cast into a dead sleep.
**76:7** Thou, even thou, art to be feared: and who may stand in thy sight when once thou art angry?
**76:8** Thou didst cause judgment to be heard from heaven; the earth feared, and was still,
**76:9 When God arose to judgment, to save all the meek of the earth. Selah.**
**76:10 Surely the wrath of man shall praise thee: the remainder of wrath shalt thou restrain.**
**76:11 Vow, and pay unto the LORD your God: let all that be round about him bring presents unto him that ought to be feared.**
**76:12** He shall cut off the spirit of princes: he is terrible to the kings of the earth.

**Psalm 77**          **11Q6**

**Psalm 77:1** I cried unto God with my voice, even unto God with my voice; and he gave ear unto me.

**77:2** In the day of my trouble I sought the Lord: my hand was stretched out in the night, and ceased not: my soul refused to be comforted.

**77:3** I remembered God, and was troubled: I complained, and my spirit was overwhelmed. Selah.

**77:4** Thou holdest mine eyes waking: I am so troubled that I cannot speak.

**77:5** I have considered the days of old, the years of ancient times.

**77:6** I call to remembrance my song in the night: I commune with mine own heart: and my spirit made diligent search.

**77:7** Will the Lord cast off for ever? And will he be favourable no more?

**77:8** Is his mercy clean gone for ever? Doth his promise fail for evermore?

**77:9** Hath God forgotten to be gracious? Hath he in anger shut up his tender mercies? Selah.

**77:10** And I said, This is my infirmity: but I will remember the years of the right hand of the most High.

**77:11** I will remember the works of the LORD: surely I will remember thy wonders of old.

**77:12** I will meditate also of all thy work, and talk of thy doings.

**77:13** Thy way, O God, is in the sanctuary: who is so great a God as our God?

**77:14** Thou art the God that doest wonders: thou hast declared thy strength among the people.

**77:15** Thou hast with thine arm redeemed thy people, the sons of Jacob and Joseph. Selah.

**77:16** The waters saw thee, O God, the waters saw thee; they were afraid: the depths also were troubled.

**77:17 The clouds poured out water: the skies sent out a sound: thine arrows also went abroad.**

**77:18 The voice of thy thunder was in the heaven: the lightnings**

lightened the world: the earth trembled and shook.
77:19 Thy way is in the sea, and thy path in the great waters, and thy footsteps are not known.
77:20 Thou led thy people like a flock by the hand of Moses and Aaron.

## Psalm 78        11Q8 & 4Q87

**Psalm 78:1** Give ear, O my people, to my law: incline your ears to the words of my mouth.

**78:2** I will open my mouth in a parable: I will utter dark sayings of old:

**78:3** Which we have heard and known, and our fathers have told us.

**78:4** We will not hide them from their children, showing to the generation to come the praises of the LORD, and his strength, and his wonderful works that he hath done.

**78:5 For he established a testimony in Jacob, and appointed a law in Israel, which he commanded our fathers, that they should make them known to their children:**

**78:6 That the generation to come might know them, even the children which should be born; who should arise and declare them to their children:**

**78:7 That they might set their hope in God, and not forget the works of God, but keep his commandments:**

**78:8 And might not be as their fathers, a stubborn and rebellious generation; a generation that set not their heart aright, and whose spirit was not stedfast with God.**

**78:9 The children of Ephraim, being armed, and carrying bows, turned back in the day of battle.**

**78:10 They kept not the covenant of God, and refused to walk in his law;**

**78:11 And forgot his works, and his wonders that he had showed them.**

**78:12 Marvellous things did he in the sight of their fathers, in the land of Egypt, in the field of Zoan.**

**78:13** He divided the sea, and caused them to pass through; and he made the waters to stand as an heap.

**78:14** In the daytime also he led them with a cloud, and all the night with a light of fire.

**78:15** He clave the rocks in the wilderness, and gave them drink as out of the great depths.

**78:16** He brought streams also out of the rock, and caused waters to run down like rivers.

**78:17** And they sinned yet more against him by provoking the most High in the wilderness.

**78:18** And they tempted God in their heart by asking food for their desire.

**78:19** Yea, they spake against God; they said, Can God furnish a table in the wilderness?

**78:20** Behold, he smote the rock, that the waters gushed out, and the streams overflowed; can he give bread also? Can he provide meat for his people?

**78:21** Therefore the LORD heard this, and was wroth: so a fire was kindled against Jacob, and anger also came up against Israel;

**78:22** Because they believed not in God, and trusted not in his salvation:

**78:23** Though he had commanded the clouds from above, and opened the doors of heaven,

**78:24** And had rained down manna upon them to eat, and had given them of the grain of heaven.

**78:25** Man did eat angels' bread: he sent them food to the full.

**78:26** He caused an east wind to blow in the heaven: and by his power he brought in the south wind.

**78:27** He rained meat also upon them as dust, and feathered fowls like as the sand of the sea:

**78:28** And he let it fall in the midst of their camp, round about their habitations.

**78:29** So they did eat, and were well filled: for he gave them their own desire;

**78:30** They were not estranged from their desire. But while their food was yet in their mouths,

**78:31 The wrath of God came upon them, and slew the fattest of them, and smote down the chosen men of Israel.**

**78:32 For all this they sinned still, and believed not for his wondrous works.**

**78:33 Therefore their days did he consume in vanity, and their years in trouble.**

**78:34** When he slew them, then they sought him: and they returned and enquired early after God.

**78:35** And they remembered that God was their rock, and the high God their redeemer.

**78:36** Nevertheless they did flatter him with their mouth, and they lied unto him with their tongues.

**78:37** For their heart was not right with him, neither were they stedfast in his covenant.

**78:38** But he, being full of compassion, forgave their iniquity, and destroyed them not: yea, many a time turned he his anger away, and did not stir up all his wrath.

**78:39** For he remembered that they were but flesh; a wind that passeth away, and cometh not again.

**78:40** How oft did they provoke him in the wilderness, and grieve him in the desert!

**78:41** Yea, they turned back and tempted God, and limited the Holy One of Israel.

**78:42** They remembered not his hand, nor the day when he delivered them from the enemy.

**78:43** How he had wrought his signs in Egypt, and his wonders in the field of Zoan.

**78:44** And had turned their rivers into blood; and their waters, that they could not drink.

**78:45** He sent diverse sorts of flies among them, which devoured them; and frogs, which destroyed them.

**78:46** He gave also their crops unto the grasshopper, and their labour unto the locust.

**78:47** He destroyed their vines with hail, and their sycomore trees with frost.

**78:48** He gave up their cattle also to the hail, and their flocks to hot thunderbolts.

**78:49** He cast upon them the fierceness of his anger, wrath, and indignation, and trouble, by sending evil angels among them.

**78:50** He made a way to his anger; he spared not their soul from death, but gave their life over to the pestilence;

**78:51** And smote all the firstborn in Egypt; the chief of their strength in the tabernacles of Ham:

**78:52** But made his own people to go forth like sheep, and guided them in the wilderness like a flock.

**78:53** And he led them on safely, so that they feared not: but the sea overwhelmed their enemies.

**78:54** And he brought them to the border of his sanctuary, even to this mountain, which his right hand had purchased.

**78:55** He cast out the nations also before them, and divided them an inheritance by line, and made the tribes of Israel to dwell in their tents.

**78:56** Yet they tempted and provoked the most high God, and kept not his testimonies:

**78:57** But turned back, and dealt unfaithfully like their fathers: they were turned aside like a deceitful bow.

**78:58** For they provoked him to anger with their high places, and moved him to jealousy with their graven images.

**78:59** When God heard this, he was wroth, and greatly abhorred Israel:

**78:60** So that he forsook the tabernacle of Shiloh, the tent which he placed among men;

**78:61** And delivered his strength into captivity, and his glory into the enemy's hand.

**78:62** He gave his people over also unto the sword; and was wroth with his inheritance.

**78:63** The fire consumed their young men; and their maidens were not given to marriage.

**78:64** Their priests fell by the sword; and their widows made no lamentation.

**78:65** Then the LORD awaked as one out of sleep, and like a mighty man that shouteth by reason of wine.

**78:66** And he smote his enemies in the hinder parts: he put them to a perpetual reproach.

**78:67** Moreover he refused the tabernacle of Joseph, and chose not the tribe of Ephraim:

**78:68** But chose the tribe of Judah, the mount Zion which he loved.

**78:69** And he built his sanctuary like high palaces, like the earth which he hath established for ever.

**78:70** He chose David also his servant, and took him from the sheepfolds:

**78:71** From following the ewes great with young he brought him to feed Jacob his people, and Israel his inheritance.

**78:72** So he fed them according to the integrity of his heart; and guided them by the skilfulness of his hands.

## Psalm 81            4Q87 & 11Q8

**Psalm 81:1 Sing aloud unto God our strength: make a joyful noise unto the God of Jacob.**

**81:2 Take a psalm, and bring hither the timbrel, the pleasant harp with the psaltery.**

**81:3 Blow the trumpet in the new moon, in the time appointed, on our solemn feast day.**

**81:4 For this was a statute for Israel, and a law of the God of Jacob.**

**81:5 This he ordained in Joseph for a testimony, when he went out through the land of Egypt: where I heard a language that I understood not.**

**81:6 I removed his shoulder from the burden: his hands were delivered from the pots.**

**81:7 Thou calledst in trouble, and I delivered thee; I answered thee in the secret place of thunder: I proved thee at the waters of Meribah.**
**Selah.**

**81:8 Hear, O my people, and I will testify unto thee: O Israel, if thou wilt hearken unto me;**

81:9 There shall no strange god be in thee; neither shalt thou worship any strange god.

81:10 I am the LORD thy God, which brought thee out of the land of Egypt: open thy mouth wide, and I will fill it.

81:11 But my people would not hearken to my voice; and Israel would have none of me.

81:12 So I gave them up unto their own hearts' desire: and they walked in their own counsels.

81:13 Oh that my people had hearkened unto me, and Israel had walked in my ways!

81:14 I should soon have subdued their enemies, and turned my hand against their adversaries.

81:15 The haters of the LORD should have submitted themselves unto him: but their time should have endured for ever.

81:16 He should have fed them also with the finest of the wheat: and with honey out of the rock should I have satisfied thee.

## Psalm 86            1Q10 & 4Q87 & 11Q8

**Psalm 86:1** Bow down thine ear, O LORD, hear me: for I am poor and needy.

**86:2** Preserve my soul; for I am holy: O thou my God, save thy servant that trusteth in thee.

**86:3** Be merciful unto me, O Lord: for I cry unto thee daily.

**86:4** Rejoice the soul of thy servant: for unto thee, O Lord, do I lift up my soul.

**86:5 For thou, Lord, art good, and ready to forgive; and plenteous in mercy unto all them that call upon thee.**

**86:6 Give ear, O LORD, unto my prayer; and attend to the voice of my supplications.**

**86:7 In the day of my trouble I will call upon thee: for thou wilt answer me.**

**86:8 Among the gods there is none like unto thee, O Lord; neither are there any works like unto thy works.**

**86:9** All nations whom thou hast made shall come and worship before thee, O Lord; and shall glorify thy name.

**86:10 For thou art great, and doest wondrous things: thou art God alone.**

**86:11 Teach me thy way, O LORD; I will walk in thy truth: unite my heart to fear thy name.**

**86:12 I will praise thee, O Lord my God, with all my heart: and I will glorify thy name for evermore.**

**86:13 For great is thy mercy toward me: and thou hast delivered my soul from the lowest hell.**

**86:14 O God, the proud are risen against me, and the assemblies of violent men have sought after my soul; and have not set thee before them.**

**86:15** But thou, O Lord, art a God full of compassion, and gracious, long suffering, and plenteous in mercy and truth.

**86:16** O turn unto me, and have mercy upon me; give thy strength unto thy servant, and save the son of thine handmaid.

**86:17** Show me a token for good; that they which hate me may see it, and be ashamed: because thou, LORD, hast helped me, and comforted me.

**Psalm 88**  **4Q87 & 4Q98(d) & 4Q98(b)**

**Psalm 88:1 O lord God of my salvation, I have cried day and night before thee:**
**88:2 Let my prayer come before thee: incline thine ear unto my cry;**
**88:3 For my soul is full of troubles: and my life draweth nigh unto the grave.**
**88:4 I am counted with them that go down into the pit: I am as a man that hath no strength:**
88:5 Free among the dead, like the slain that lay in the grave, whom thou rememberest no more: and they are cut off from thy hand.
88:6 Thou hast laid me in the lowest pit, in darkness, in the deeps.
88:7 Thy wrath layeth hard upon me, and thou hast afflicted me with all thy waves. Selah.
88:8 Thou hast put away mine acquaintance far from me; thou hast made me an abomination unto them: I am shut up, and I cannot come forth.
88:9 Mine eye mourneth by reason of affliction: LORD, I have called daily upon thee, I have stretched out my hands unto thee.
88:10 Wilt thou show wonders to the dead? Shall the dead arise and praise thee? Selah.
**88:11 Shall thy lovingkindness be declared in the grave? Or thy faithfulness in destruction?**
88:12 Shall thy wonders be known in the dark? And thy righteousness in the land of forgetfulness?
88:13 But unto thee have I cried, O LORD; and in the morning shall my prayer meet thee.
**88:14 LORD, why castest thou off my soul? Why hidest thou thy face from me?**
**88:15 I am afflicted and ready to die from my youth up: while I suffer thy terrors I am distracted.**
**88:16 Thy fierce wrath goeth over me; thy terrors have cut me off.**
88:17 They came round about me daily like water; they compassed me about together.

**88:18** Lover and friend hast thou put far from me, and mine acquaintance into darkness.

## Psalm 89          4Q87

**Psalm 89:1** I will sing of the mercies of the LORD for ever: with my mouth will I make known thy faithfulness to all generations. **89:2** For I have said, Mercy shall be built up for ever: thy faithfulness shalt thou establish in the very heavens. **89:3** I have made a covenant with my chosen, I have sworn unto David my servant, **89:4** Thy descendants will I establish for ever, and build up thy throne to all generations. Selah. **89:5** And the heavens shall praise thy wonders, O LORD: thy faithfulness also in the congregation of the saints. **89:6** For who in the heaven can be compared unto the LORD? Who among the sons of the mighty can be likened unto the LORD? **89:7** God is greatly to be feared in the assembly of the saints, and to be had in reverence of all them that are about him. **89:8** O LORD God of armies, who is a strong LORD like unto thee? Or to thy faithfulness round about thee? **89:9** Thou rulest the raging of the sea: when the waves thereof arise, thou stillest them. **89:10** Thou hast broken Rahab in pieces, as one that is slain; thou hast scattered thine enemies with thy strong arm. **89:11** The heavens are thine, the earth also is thine: as for the world and the fulness thereof, thou hast founded them. **89:12** The north and the south thou hast created them: Tabor and Hermon shall rejoice in thy name. **89:13** Thou hast a mighty arm: strong is thy hand, and high is thy right hand. **89:14** Justice and judgment are the habitation of thy throne: mercy and truth shall go before thy face. **89:15** Blessed is the people that know the joyful sound: they shall walk, O LORD, in the light of thy countenance. **89:16** In thy name shall they rejoice all the day: and in thy righteousness shall they be exalted. **89:17** For thou art the glory of their strength: and in thy favour our horn shall be exalted.

**89:18** For the LORD is our defense; and the Holy One of Israel is our king.

**89:19** Then thou spakest in vision to thy holy one, and saidst, I have laid help upon one that is mighty; I have exalted one chosen out of the people.

**89:20** I have found David my servant; with my holy oil have I anointed him:

**89:21** With whom my hand shall be established: mine arm also shall strengthen him.

**89:22** The enemy shall not exact upon him; nor the son of wickedness afflict him.

**89:23** And I will beat down his foes before his face, and plague them that hate him.

**89:24** But my faithfulness and my mercy shall be with him: and in my name shall his horn be exalted.

**89:25** I will set his hand also in the sea, and his right hand in the rivers.

**89:26** He shall cry unto me, Thou art my father, my God, and the rock of my salvation.

**89:27** Also I will make him my firstborn, higher than the kings of the earth.

**89:28** My mercy will I keep for him for evermore, and my covenant shall stand fast with him.

**89:29** His descendants also will I make to endure for ever, and his throne as the days of heaven.

**89:30** If his children forsake my law, and walk not in my judgments;

**89:31** If they break my statutes, and keep not my commandments;

**89:32** Then will I visit their transgression with the rod, and their iniquity with stripes.

**89:33** Nevertheless my lovingkindness will I not utterly take from him, nor suffer my faithfulness to fail.

**89:34** My covenant will I not break, nor alter the thing that is gone out of my lips.

**89:35** Once have I sworn by my holiness that I will not lie unto David.

**89:36** His descendants shall endure for ever, and his throne as the sun before me.

**89:37** It shall be established for ever as the moon, and as a faithful witness in heaven. Selah.

**89:38** But thou hast cast off and abhorred, thou hast been wroth with thine anointed.

**89:39** Thou hast made void the covenant of thy servant: thou hast profaned his crown by casting it to the ground.

**89:40** Thou hast broken down all his hedges; thou hast brought his strong holds to ruin.

**89:41** All that pass by the way plunder him: he is a reproach to his neighbours.

**89:42** Thou hast set up the right hand of his adversaries; thou hast made all his enemies to rejoice.

**89:43 Thou hast also turned the edge of his sword, and hast not made him to stand in the battle.**

**89:44 Thou hast made his glory to cease, and cast his throne down to the ground.**

**89:45 The days of his youth hast thou shortened: thou hast covered him with shame. Selah.**

**89:46 How long, LORD? Wilt thou hide thyself for ever? Shall thy wrath burn like fire?**

**89:47 Remember how short my time is: wherefore hast thou made all men in vain?**

**89:48** What man is he that liveth, and shall not see death? Shall he deliver his soul from the hand of the grave? Selah.

**89:49 Lord, where are thy former lovingkindnesses, which thou swarest unto David in thy truth?**

**89:50 Remember, Lord, the reproach of thy servants; how I do bear in my bosom the reproach of all the mighty people;**

**89:51 Wherewith thine enemies have reproached, O LORD; wherewith they have reproached the footsteps of thine anointed.**

**89:52 Blessed be the LORD for evermore. Amen, and Amen.**

**Psalm 91**     **4Q84**

**Psalm 91:1** He that dwelleth in the secret place of the most High shall abide under the shadow of the Almighty.

**91:2** I will say of the LORD, He is my refuge and my fortress: my God; in him will I trust.

**91:3** Surely he shall deliver thee from the snare of the fowler, and from the noisome pestilence.

**91:4** He shall cover thee with his feathers, and under his wings shalt thou trust: his truth shall be thy shield and buckler.

**91:5 Thou shalt not be afraid for the terror by night; nor for the arrow that flieth by day;**

**91:6 Nor for the pestilence that walketh in darkness; nor for the destruction that wasteth at noonday.**

**91:7 A thousand shall fall at thy side, and ten thousand at thy right hand; but it shall not come nigh thee.**

**91:8 Only with thine eyes shalt thou behold and see the reward of the wicked.**

**91:9** Because thou hast made the LORD, which is my refuge, even the most High, thy habitation;

**91:10** There shall no evil befall thee, neither shall any plague come nigh thy dwelling.

**91:11** For he shall give his angels charge over thee, to keep thee in all thy ways.

**91:12 They shall bear thee up in their hands, lest thou dash thy foot against a stone.**

**91:13 Thou shalt tread upon the lion and adder: the young lion and the dragon shalt thou trample under feet.**

**91:14 Because he hath set his love upon me, therefore will I deliver him: I will set him on high, because he hath known my name.**

**91:15 He shall call upon me, and I will answer him: I will be with him in trouble; I will deliver him, and honour him.**

**91:16** With long life will I satisfy him, and show him my salvation.

**Psalm 92**  **4Q84 & 1Q10**

**Psalm 92:1** IT IS A GOOD THING TO GIVE THANKS UNTO THE LORD, AND TO SING PRAISES UNTO THY NAME, O MOST HIGH:
**92:2** To show forth thy lovingkindness in the morning, and thy faithfulness every night,
**92:3 Upon an instrument of ten strings, and upon the psaltery; upon the harp with a solemn sound.**
**92:4 For thou, LORD, hast made me glad through thy work: I will triumph in the works of thy hands.**
**92:5 O LORD, how great are thy works! And thy thoughts are very deep.**
**92:6 A brutish man knoweth not; neither doth a fool understand this.**
**92:7 When the wicked spring as the grass, and when all the workers of iniquity do flourish; it is that they shall be destroyed for ever:**
**92:8** But thou, LORD, art most high for evermore.
**92:9** For, lo, thine enemies, O LORD, for, lo, thine enemies shall perish; all the workers of iniquity shall be scattered.
**92:10** But my horn shalt thou exalt like the horn of an unicorn: I shall be anointed with fresh oil.
**92:11 Mine eye also shall see my desire on mine enemies, and mine ears shall hear my desire of the wicked that rise up against me.**
**92:12 The righteous shall flourish like the palm tree: he shall grow like a cedar in Lebanon.**
**92:13 Those that be planted in the house of the LORD shall flourish in the courts of our God.**
**92:14 They shall still bring forth fruit in old age; they shall be fat and flourishing;**
**92:15** To show that the LORD is upright: he is my rock, and there is no unrighteousness in him.

**Psalm 93**           **11Q5 & 4Q94**

**Psalm 93:1 The LORD reigneth, he is clothed with majesty; the LORD is clothed with strength, wherewith he hath girded himself: the world also is stablished, that it cannot be moved. 93:2 Thy throne is established of old: thou art from everlasting. 93:3 The floods have lifted up, O LORD, the floods have lifted up their voice; the floods lift up their waves. 93:4 The LORD on high is mightier than the noise of many waters, yea, than the mighty waves of the sea. 93:5 Thy testimonies are very sure: holiness becometh thine house, O LORD, for ever.**

**Psalm 94**              **4Q84 & 1Q10**

**Psalm 94:1 O LORD God, to whom vengeance belongeth; O God, to whom vengeance belongeth, show thyself.**
**94:2 Lift up thyself, thou judge of the earth: render a reward to the proud.**
**94:3 LORD, how long shall the wicked, how long shall the wicked triumph?**
**94:4 How long shall they utter and speak hard things? And all the workers of iniquity boast themselves?**
**94:5** They break in pieces thy people, O LORD, and afflict thine heritage.
**94:6** They slay the widow and the stranger, and murder the fatherless.
**94:7** Yet they say, The LORD shall not see, neither shall the God of Jacob regard it.
**94:8 Understand, ye brutish among the people: and ye fools, when will ye be wise?**
**94:9 He that planted the ear, shall he not hear? He that formed the eye, shall he not see?**
**94:10 He that chastiseth the nations, shall not he correct? He that teacheth man knowledge, shall not he know?**
**94:11 The LORD knoweth the thoughts of man, that they are vanity.**
**94:12 Blessed is the man whom thou chastenest, O LORD, and teachest him out of thy law;**
**94:13 That thou mayest give him rest from the days of adversity, until the pit be digged for the wicked.**
**94:14 For the LORD will not cast off his people, neither will he forsake his inheritance.**
**94:15** But judgment shall return unto righteousness: and all the upright in heart shall follow it.
**94:16 Who will rise up for me against the evildoers? Or who will stand up for me against the workers of iniquity?**
**94:17 Unless the LORD had been my help, my soul had almost dwelt in silence.**

**94:18 When I said, My foot slippeth; thy mercy, O LORD, held me up.**

94:19 In the multitude of my thoughts within me thy comforts delight my soul.

94:20 Shall the throne of iniquity have fellowship with thee, which frameth mischief by a law?

**94:21 They gather themselves together against the soul of the righteous, and condemn the innocent blood.**

**94:22 But the LORD is my defense; and my God is the rock of my refuge.**

94:23 And he shall bring upon them their own iniquity, and shall cut them off in their own wickedness; yea, the LORD our God shall cut them off.

## Psalm 95          4Q94 & 1Q10

**Psalm 95:1** O come, let us sing unto the LORD: let us make a joyful noise to the rock of our salvation.

**95:2** Let us come before his presence with thanksgiving, and make a joyful noise unto him with psalms.

**95:3 For the LORD is a great God, and a great King above all gods.**

**95:4 In his hand are the deep places of the earth: the strength of the hills is his also.**

**95:5 The sea is his, and he made it: and his hands formed the dry land.**

**95:6 O come, let us worship and bow down: let us kneel before the LORD our maker.**

**95:7** For he is our God; and we are the people of his pasture, and the sheep of his hand. To day if ye will hear his voice,

**95:8** Harden not your heart, as in the provocation, and as in the day of temptation in the wilderness:

**95:9** When your fathers tempted me, proved me, and saw my work.

**95:10** Forty years long was I grieved with this generation, and said, It is a people that do err in their heart, and they have not known my ways:

**95:11 Unto whom I sware in my wrath that they should not enter into my rest.**

**Psalm 97**          **4Q94**

**Psalm 97:1** The LORD reigneth; let the earth rejoice; let the multitude of isles be glad thereof.
**97:2** Clouds and darkness are round about him: righteousness and judgment are the habitation of his throne.
**97:3** A fire goeth before him, and burneth up his enemies round about.
**97:4** His lightnings enlightened the world: the earth saw, and trembled.
**97:5** The hills melted like wax at the presence of the LORD, at the presence of the Lord of the whole earth.
**97:6 The heavens declare his righteousness, and all the people see his glory.**
**97:7 Confounded be all they that serve graven images, that boast themselves of idols: worship him, all ye gods.**
**97:8 Zion heard, and was glad; and the daughters of Judah rejoiced because of thy judgments, O LORD.**
**97:9 For thou, LORD, art high above all the earth: thou art exalted far above all gods.**
**97:10** Ye that love the LORD, hate evil: he preserveth the souls of his saints; he delivereth them out of the hand of the wicked.
**97:11** Light is sown for the righteous, and gladness for the upright in heart.
**97:12** Rejoice in the LORD, ye righteous; and give thanks at the remembrance of his holiness.

**Psalm 98**          **4Q94**

**Psalm 98:1** O sing unto the LORD a new song; for he hath done marvellous things: his right hand, and his holy arm, hath gotten him the victory.
**98:2** The LORD hath made known his salvation: his righteousness hath he openly showed in the sight of the nations.
**98:3** He hath remembered his mercy and his truth toward the house of Israel: all the ends of the earth have seen the salvation of our God.
**98:4 Make a joyful noise unto the LORD, all the earth: make a loud noise, and rejoice, and sing praise.**
**98:5 Sing unto the LORD with the harp; with the harp, and the voice of a psalm.**
**98:6 With trumpets and sound of cornet make a joyful noise before the LORD, the King.**
**98:7 Let the sea roar, and the fulness thereof; the world, and they that dwell therein.**
**98:8 Let the floods clap their hands: let the hills be joyful together**
**98:9** Before the LORD; for he cometh to judge the earth: with righteousness shall he judge the world, and the people with equity.

## Psalm 99        4Q92 & 4Q84

**Psalm 99:1 The LORD reigneth; let the people tremble: he is seated between the cherubims; let the earth be moved.**
**99:2 The LORD is great in Zion; and he is high above all the people.**
**99:3 Let them praise thy great and awesome name; for it is holy.**
**99:4 The king's strength also loveth judgment; thou dost establish equity, thou executest judgment and righteousness in Jacob.**
**99:5 Exalt ye the LORD our God, and worship at his footstool; for he is holy.**
**99:6 Moses and Aaron among his priests, and Samuel among them that call upon his name; they called upon the LORD, and he answered them.**
99:7 He spake unto them in the cloudy pillar: they kept his testimonies, and the ordinance that he gave them.
99:8 Thou answeredst them, O LORD our God: thou wast a God that forgavest them, though thou tookest vengeance of their inventions.
99:9 Exalt the LORD our God, and worship at his holy hill; for the LORD our God is holy.

**Psalm 100**          **4Q84**

**Psalm 100:1 Make a joyful noise unto the LORD, all ye lands.
100:2 Serve the LORD with gladness: come before his presence
with singing.**
**100:3** Know ye that the LORD he is God: it is he that hath made us,
and not we ourselves; we are his people, and the sheep of his
pasture.
**100:4** Enter into his gates with thanksgiving, and into his courts
with praise: be thankful unto him, and bless his name.
**100:5** For the LORD is good; his mercy is everlasting; and his truth
endureth to all generations.

**Psalm 101**         **11Q5**

**Psalm 101:1 I will sing of mercy and judgment: unto thee, O LORD, will I sing.**
**101:2 I will behave myself wisely in a perfect way. O when wilt thou come unto me? I will walk within my house with a perfect heart.**
**101:3 I will set no wicked thing before mine eyes: I hate the work of them that turn aside; it shall not cleave to me.**
**101:4 A froward heart shall depart from me: I will not know a wicked person.**
**101:5 Whoso privily slandereth his neighbour, him will I cut off: him that hath an high look and a proud heart will not I suffer.**
**101:6 Mine eyes shall be upon the faithful of the land, that they may dwell with me: he that walketh in a perfect way, he shall serve me.**
**101:7 He that worketh deceit shall not dwell within my house: he that telleth lies shall not tarry in my sight.**
**101:8 I will early destroy all the wicked of the land; that I may cut off all wicked doers from the city of the LORD.**

## Psalm 102          4Q84 & 11Q5

**Psalm 102:1** Hear my prayer, O LORD, and let my cry come unto thee.

**102:2** Hide not thy face from me in the day when I am in trouble; incline thine ear unto me: in the day when I call answer me speedily.

**102:3** For my days are consumed like smoke, and my bones are burned as an hearth.

**102:4** My heart is stricken, and withered like grass; so that I forget to eat my bread.

**102:5** By reason of the voice of my groaning my bones cleave to my skin.

**102:6** I am like a pelican of the wilderness: I am like an owl of the desert.

**102:7** I watch, and am as a sparrow alone upon the house top.

**102:8** Mine enemies reproach me all the day; and they that are mad against me are sworn against me.

**102:9 For I have eaten ashes like bread, and mingled my drink with weeping.**

**102:10 Because of thine indignation and thy wrath: for thou hast lifted me up, and cast me down.**

**102:11 My days are like a shadow that declineth; and I am withered like grass.**

**102:12 But thou, O LORD, shall endure for ever; and thy remembrance unto all generations.**

**102:13 Thou shalt arise, and have mercy upon Zion: for the time to favour her, yea, the set time, is come.**

**102:14 For thy servants take pleasure in her stones, and favour the dust thereof.**

**102:15 So the nations shall fear the name of the LORD, and all the kings of the earth thy glory.**

**102:16 When the LORD shall build up Zion, he shall appear in his glory.**

**102:17 He will regard the prayer of the destitute, and not despise their prayer.**

**102:18 This shall be written for the generation to come: and the**

people which shall be created shall praise the LORD.

102:19 For he hath looked down from the height of his sanctuary; from heaven did the LORD behold the earth;

102:20 To hear the groaning of the prisoner; to loose those that are appointed to death;

102:21 To declare the name of the LORD in Zion, and his praise in Jerusalem;

102:22 When the people are gathered together, and the kingdoms, to serve the LORD.

102:23 He weakened my strength in the way; he shortened my days.

102:24 I said, O my God, take me not away in the midst of my days: thy years are throughout all generations.

102:25 Of old hast thou laid the foundation of the earth: and the heavens are the work of thy hands.

102:26 They shall perish, but thou shalt endure: yea, all of them shall wax old like a garment; as a vesture shalt thou change them, and they shall be changed:

102:27 But thou art the same, and thy years shall have no end.

102:28 The children of thy servants shall continue, and their descendants shall be established before thee.

## Psalm 103　　　4Q84

**Psalm 103:1** Bless the LORD, O my soul: and all that is within me, bless his holy name.
**103:2** Bless the LORD, O my soul, and forget not all his benefits:
**103:3** Who forgiveth all thine iniquities; who healeth all thy diseases;
**103:4 Who redeemeth thy life from destruction; who crowneth thee with lovingkindness and tender mercies;**
**103:5 Who satisfieth thy mouth with good things; so that thy youth is renewed like the eagle's.**
**103:6 The LORD executeth righteousness and judgment for all that are oppressed.**
**103:7** He made known his ways unto Moses, his acts unto the children of Israel.
**103:8** The LORD is merciful and gracious, slow to anger, and plenteous in mercy.
**103:9 He will not always chide: neither will he keep his anger for ever.**
**103:10 He hath not dealt with us after our sins; nor rewarded us according to our iniquities.**
**103:11 For as the heaven is high above the earth, so great is his mercy toward them that fear him.**
**103:12 As far as the east is from the west, so far hath he removed our transgressions from us.**
**103:13 Like as a father pitieth his children, so the LORD pitieth them that fear him.**
**103:14 For he knoweth our frame; he remembereth that we are dust.**
**103:15** As for man, his days are as grass: as a flower of the field, so he flourisheth.
**103:16** For the wind passeth over it, and it is gone; and the place thereof shall know it no more.
**103:17** But the mercy of the LORD is from everlasting to everlasting upon them that fear him, and his righteousness unto children's children;

**103:18** To such as keep his covenant, and to those that remember his commandments to do them.

**103:19** The LORD hath prepared his throne in the heavens; and his kingdom ruleth over all.

**103:20 Bless the LORD, ye his angels, that excel in strength, that do his commandments, hearkening unto the voice of his word.**

**103:21 Bless ye the LORD, all ye his hosts; ye ministers of his, that do his pleasure.**

**103:22** Bless the LORD, all his works in all places of his dominion: bless the LORD, O my soul.

**Psalm 104**　　　　**4Q86 & 4Q87 & 4Q93 & 11Q5**

**Psalm 104:1 Bless the LORD, O my soul. O LORD my God, thou art very great; thou art clothed with honour and majesty. 104:2 Who coverest thyself with light as with a garment: who stretchest out the heavens like a curtain: 104:3 Who layeth the beams of his chambers in the waters: who maketh the clouds his chariot: who walketh upon the wings of the wind: 104:4 Who maketh his angels spirits; his ministers a flaming fire: 104:5 Who laid the foundations of the earth, that it should not be removed for ever. 104:6 Thou coveredst it with the deep as with a garment: the waters stood above the mountains.**
104:7 At thy rebuke they fled; at the voice of thy thunder they hasted away. **104:8 They go up by the mountains; they go down by the valleys unto the place which thou hast founded for them. 104:9 Thou hast set a bound that they may not pass over; that they turn not again to cover the earth. 104:10 He sendeth the springs into the valleys, which run among the hills. 104:11 They give drink to every beast of the field: the wild asses quench their thirst. 104:12 By them shall the fowls of the heaven have their habitation, which sing among the branches.** 104:13 He watereth the hills from his chambers: the earth is satisfied with the fruit of thy works. **104:14 He causeth the grass to grow for the cattle, and herb for the service of man: that he may bring forth food out of the earth; 104:15 And wine that maketh glad the heart of man, and oil to make his face to shine, and bread which strengtheneth man's heart.** 104:16 The trees of the LORD are full of sap; the cedars of

Lebanon, which he hath planted;

**104:17** Where the birds make their nests: as for the stork, the fir trees are her house.

**104:18** The high hills are a refuge for the wild goats; and the rocks for the rabbits.

**104:19** He appointed the moon for seasons: the sun knoweth his going down.

**104:20** Thou makest darkness, and it is night: wherein all the beasts of the forest do roam forth.

**104:21** The young lions roar after their prey, and seek their food from God.

**104:22 The sun ariseth, they gather themselves together, and lay them down in their dens.**

**104:23 Man goeth forth unto his work and to his labour until the evening.**

**104:24 O LORD, how manifold are thy works! In wisdom hast thou made them all: the earth is full of thy riches.**

**104:25 So is this great and wide sea, wherein are things roaming innumerable, both small and great living creatures.**

**104:26 There go the ships: there is that leviathan, whom thou hast made to play therein.**

**104:27 These wait all upon thee; that thou mayest give them their food in due season.**

**104:28 That thou givest them they gather: thou openest thine hand, they are filled with good.**

**104:29 Thou hidest thy face, they are troubled: thou takest away their breath, they die, and return to their dust.**

**104:30 Thou sendest forth thy spirit, they are created: and thou renewest the face of the earth.**

**104:31 The glory of the LORD shall endure for ever: the LORD shall rejoice in his works.**

**104:32 He looketh on the earth, and it trembleth: he toucheth the hills, and they smoke.**

**104:33 I will sing unto the LORD as long as I live: I will sing praise to my God while I have my being.**

**104:34 My meditation of him shall be sweet: I will be glad in the**

**LORD.**
**104:35 Let the sinners be consumed out of the earth, and let the wicked be no more. Bless thou the LORD, O my soul. Praise ye the LORD.**

## Psalm 105          4Q87 & 11Q5

**Psalm 105:1** O give thanks unto the LORD; call upon his name: make known his deeds among the people.

**105:2** Sing unto him, sing psalms unto him: talk ye of all his wondrous works.

**105:3** Glory ye in his holy name: let the heart of them rejoice that seek the LORD.

**105:4** Seek the LORD, and his strength: seek his face evermore.

**105:5** Remember his marvellous works that he hath done; his wonders, and the judgments of his mouth;

**105:6** O ye descendants of Abraham his servant, ye children of Jacob his chosen.

**105:7** He is the LORD our God: his judgments are in all the earth.

**105:8** He hath remembered his covenant for ever, the word which he commanded to a thousand generations.

**105:9** Which covenant he made with Abraham, and his oath unto Isaac;

**105:10** And confirmed the same unto Jacob for a law, and to Israel for an everlasting covenant:

**105:11** Saying, Unto thee will I give the land of Canaan, the lot of your inheritance:

**105:12** When they were but a few men in number; yea, very few, and strangers in it.

**105:13** When they went from one nation to another, from one kingdom to another people;

**105:14** He suffered no man to do them wrong: yea, he reproved kings for their sakes;

**105:15** Saying, Touch not mine anointed, and do my prophets no harm.

**105:16** Moreover he called for a famine upon the land: he brake the whole staff of bread.

**105:17** He sent a man before them, even Joseph, who was sold for a servant:

**105:18** Whose feet they hurt with fetters: he was laid in iron:

**105:19** Until the time that his word came: the word of the LORD tried him.

**105:20** The king sent and loosed him; even the ruler of the people, and let him go free.

**105:21** He made him lord of his house, and ruler of all his substance:

**105:22** To bind his princes at his pleasure; and teach his senators wisdom.

**105:23 Israel also came into Egypt; and Jacob sojourned in the land of Ham.**

**105:24 And he increased his people greatly; and made them stronger than their enemies.**

**105:25 He turned their heart to hate his people, to deal subtilly with his servants.**

**105:26 He sent Moses his servant; and Aaron whom he had chosen.**

**105:27 They showed his signs among them, and wonders in the land of Ham.**

**105:28 He sent darkness, and made it dark; and they rebelled not against his word.**

**105:29 He turned their waters into blood, and slew their fish.**

**105:30 Their land brought forth frogs in abundance, in the chambers of their kings.**

**105:31 He spake, and there came diverse sorts of flies, and lice in all their coasts.**

**105:32 He gave them hail for rain, and flaming fire in their land.**

**105:33 He smote their vines also and their fig trees; and brake the trees of their coasts.**

**105:34 He spake, and the locusts came, and grasshoppers, and that without number,**

**105:35 And did eat up all the herbs in their land, and devoured the fruit of their ground.**

**105:36 He smote also all the firstborn in their land, the chief of all their strength.**

**105:37 He brought them forth also with silver and gold: and there was not one feeble person among their tribes.**

105:38 Egypt was glad when they departed: for the fear of them fell upon them.

105:39 He spread a cloud for a covering; and fire to give light in the night.

105:40 The people asked, and he brought quails, and satisfied them with the bread of heaven.

105:41 He opened the rock, and the waters gushed out; they ran in the dry places like a river.

105:42 For he remembered his holy promise, and Abraham his servant.

105:43 And he brought forth his people with joy, and his chosen with gladness:

105:44 And gave them the lands of the nations: and they inherited the labour of the people;

105:45 That they might observe his statutes, and keep his laws. Praise ye the LORD.

**Psalm 107**        **4Q88**

**Psalm 107:1** O give thanks unto the LORD, for he is good: for his mercy endureth for ever.
**107:2 Let the redeemed of the LORD say so, whom he hath redeemed from the hand of the enemy;**
**107:3 And gathered them out of the lands, from the east, and from the west, from the north, and from the south.**
**107:4 They wandered in the wilderness in a solitary way; they found no city to dwell in.**
**107:5 Hungry and thirsty, their soul fainted in them.**
**107:6** Then they cried unto the LORD in their trouble, and he delivered them out of their distresses.
**107:7** And he led them forth by the right way, that they might go to a city of habitation.
**107:8 Oh that men would praise the LORD for his goodness, and for his wonderful works to the children of men!**
**107:9 For he satisfieth the longing soul, and filleth the hungry soul with goodness.**
**107:10 Such as are seated in darkness and in the shadow of death, being bound in affliction and iron;**
**107:11 Because they rebelled against the words of God, and contemned the counsel of the most High:**
**107:12 Therefore he brought down their heart with labour; they fell down, and there was none to help.**
**107:13 Then they cried unto the LORD in their trouble, and he saved them out of their distresses.**
**107:14 He brought them out of darkness and the shadow of death, and brake their bands in sunder.**
**107:15 Oh that men would praise the LORD for his goodness, and for his wonderful works to the children of men!**
**107:16 For he hath broken the gates of bronze, and cut the bars of iron in sunder.**
**107:17** Fools because of their transgression, and because of their iniquities, are afflicted.
**107:18 Their soul abhorreth all manner of food; and they draw**

near unto the gates of death.

**107:19 Then they cry unto the LORD in their trouble, and he saveth them out of their distresses.**

107:20 He sent his word, and healed them, and delivered them from their destructions.

107:21 Oh that men would praise the LORD for his goodness, and for his wonderful works to the children of men!

**107:22 And let them sacrifice the sacrifices of thanksgiving, and declare his works with rejoicing.**

**107:23 They that go down to the sea in ships, that do business in great waters;**

**107:24 These see the works of the LORD, and his wonders in the deep.**

**107:25 For he commandeth, and raiseth the stormy wind, which lifteth up the waves thereof.**

**107:26 They mount up to the heaven, they go down again to the depths: their soul is melted because of trouble.**

**107:27 They reel to and fro, and stagger like a drunken man, and are at their wit's end.**

**107:28 Then they cry unto the LORD in their trouble, and he bringeth them out of their distresses.**

**107:29 He maketh the storm a calm, so that the waves thereof are still.**

**107:30 Then are they glad because they be quiet; so he bringeth them unto their desired haven.**

**107:31 Oh that men would praise the LORD for his goodness, and for his wonderful works to the children of men!**

**107:32 Let them exalt him also in the congregation of the people,** and praise him in the assembly of the elders.

107:33 He turneth rivers into a wilderness, and the watersprings into dry ground;

107:34 A fruitful land into barrenness, for the wickedness of them that dwell therein.

**107:35 He turneth the wilderness into a standing water, and dry ground into watersprings.**

**107:36 And there he maketh the hungry to dwell, that they may**

prepare a city for habitation;

**107:37 And sow the fields, and plant vineyards, which may yield fruits of increase.**

**107:38 He blesseth them also, so that they are multiplied greatly; and suffereth not their cattle to decrease.**

**107:39 Again, they are diminished and brought low through oppression, affliction, and sorrow.**

**107:40 He poureth contempt upon princes, and causeth them to wander in the wilderness, where there is no way.**

**107:41 Yet setteth he the poor on high from affliction, and maketh him families like a flock.**

**107:42 The righteous shall see it, and rejoice: and all iniquity shall stop her mouth.**

**107:43** Whoso is wise, and will observe these things, even they shall understand the lovingkindness of the LORD.

**Psalm 109**         **4Q88 & 11Q5**

**Psalm 109:1** Hold not thy peace, O God of my praise;
**109:2** For the mouth of the wicked and the mouth of the deceitful are opened against me: they have spoken against me with a lying tongue.
**109:3** They compassed me about also with words of hatred; and fought against me without a cause.
**109:4 For my love they are my adversaries: but I give myself unto prayer.**
**109:5 And they have rewarded me evil for good, and hatred for my love.**
**109:6 Set thou a wicked man over him: and let Satan stand at his right hand.**
**109:7** When he shall be judged, let him be condemned: and let his prayer become sin.
**109:8** Let his days be few; and let another take his office.
**109:9** Let his children be fatherless, and his wife a widow.
**109:10** Let his children be continually vagabonds, and beg: let them seek their bread also out of their desolate places.
**109:11** Let the extortioner catch all that he hath; and let the strangers plunder his labour.
**109:12** Let there be none to extend mercy unto him: neither let there be any to favour his fatherless children.
**109:13** Let his posterity be cut off; and in the generation following let their name be blotted out.
**109:14** Let the iniquity of his fathers be remembered with the LORD; and let not the sin of his mother be blotted out.
**109:15** Let them be before the LORD continually, that he may cut off the memory of them from the earth.
**109:16** Because that he remembered not to show mercy, but persecuted the poor and needy man, that he might even slay the broken in heart.
**109:17** As he loved cursing, so let it come unto him: as he delighted not in blessing, so let it be far from him.
**109:18** As he clothed himself with cursing like as with his garment,

so let it come into his belly like water, and like oil into his bones.

**109:19** Let it be unto him as the garment which covereth him, and for a girdle wherewith he is girded continually.

**109:20** Let this be the reward of mine adversaries from the LORD, and of them that speak evil against my soul.

**109:21 But do thou for me, O GOD the Lord, for thy name's sake: because thy mercy is good, deliver thou me.**

**109:22 For I am poor and needy, and my heart is wounded within me.**

**109:23 I am gone like the shadow when it declineth: I am tossed up and down as the locust.**

**109:24 My knees are weak through fasting; and my flesh faileth of fatness.**

**109:25 I became also a reproach unto them: when they looked upon me they shaked their heads.**

**109:26 Help me, O LORD my God: O save me according to thy mercy:**

**109:27 That they may know that this is thy hand; that thou, LORD, hast done it.**

**109:28 Let them curse, but bless thou: when they arise, let them be ashamed; but let thy servant rejoice.**

**109:29 Let mine adversaries be clothed with shame, and let them cover themselves with their own confusion, as with a mantle.**

**109:30 I will greatly praise the LORD with my mouth; yea, I will praise him among the multitude.**

**109:31 For he shall stand at the right hand of the poor, to save him from those that condemn his soul.**

**Psalm 112**          **4Q84**

**Psalm 112:1** Praise ye the LORD. Blessed is the man that feareth the LORD, that delighteth greatly in his commandments.

**112:2** His descendants shall be mighty upon earth: the generation of the upright shall be blessed.

**112:3** Wealth and riches shall be in his house: and his righteousness endureth for ever.

**112:4 Unto the upright there ariseth light in the darkness: he is gracious, and full of compassion, and righteous.**

**112:5 A good man showeth favour, and lendeth: he will guide his affairs with discretion.**

**112:6** Surely he shall not be moved for ever: the righteous shall be in everlasting remembrance.

**112:7** He shall not be afraid of evil tidings: his heart is fixed, trusting in the LORD.

**112:8** His heart is established, he shall not be afraid, until he see his desire upon his enemies.

**112:9** He hath dispersed, he hath given to the poor; his righteousness endureth for ever; his horn shall be exalted with honour.

**112:10** The wicked shall see it, and be grieved; he shall gnash with his teeth, and melt away: the desire of the wicked shall perish.

## Psalm 114          4Q96

**Psalm 114:1** When Israel went out of Egypt, the house of Jacob from a people of strange language;
**114:2** Judah was his sanctuary, and Israel his dominion.
**114:3** The sea saw it, and fled: Jordan was driven back.
**114:4** The mountains skipped like rams, and the little hills like lambs.
**114:5** What ailed thee, O thou sea, that thou fleddest? Thou Jordan, that thou wast driven back?
**114:6** Ye mountains, that ye skipped like rams; and ye little hills, like lambs?
**114:7 Tremble, thou earth, at the presence of the Lord, at the presence of the God of Jacob;**
**114:8 Which turned the rock into a standing water, the flint into a fountain of waters.**

## Psalm 115          4Q96 & 4Q87 & 11Q8

**Psalm 115:1 Not unto us, O LORD, not unto us, but unto thy name give glory, for thy mercy, and for thy truth's sake.**
**115:2 Wherefore should the heathen say, Where is now their God?**
**115:3 But our God is in the heavens: he hath done whatsoever he hath pleased.**
**115:4 Their idols are silver and gold, the work of men's hands.**
115:5 They have mouths, but they speak not: eyes have they, but they see not:
115:6 They have ears, but they hear not: noses have they, but they smell not:
115:7 They have hands, but they handle not: feet have they, but they walk not: neither speak they through their throat.
115:8 They that make them are like unto them; so is every one that trusteth in them.
115:9 O Israel, trust thou in the LORD: he is their help and their shield.
115:10 O house of Aaron, trust in the LORD: he is their help and their shield.
115:11 Ye that fear the LORD, trust in the LORD: he is their help and their shield.
115:12 The LORD hath been mindful of us: he will bless us; he will bless the house of Israel; he will bless the house of Aaron.
115:13 He will bless them that fear the LORD, both small and great.
115:14 The LORD shall increase you more and more, you and your children.
**115:15 Ye are blessed of the LORD which made heaven and earth.**
**115:16 The heaven, even the heavens, are the LORD's: but the earth hath he given to the children of men.**
**115:17 The dead praise not the LORD, neither any that go down into silence.**
**115:18 But we will bless the LORD from this time forth and for evermore. Praise the LORD.**

# Dead Sea Scrolls Psalms

## Psalm 116          4Q96 & 4Q84

**Psalm 116:1** I love the LORD, because he hath heard my voice and my supplications.

**116:2** Because he hath inclined his ear unto me, therefore will I call upon him as long as I live.

**116:3** The sorrows of death compassed me, and the pains of hell got hold upon me: I found trouble and sorrow.

**116:4** Then called I upon the name of the LORD; O LORD, I beseech thee, deliver my soul.

**116:5 Gracious is the LORD, and righteous; yea, our God is merciful.**

**116:6 The LORD preserveth the simple: I was brought low, and he helped me.**

**116:7 Return unto thy rest, O my soul; for the LORD hath dealt bountifully with thee.**

**116:8 For thou hast delivered my soul from death, mine eyes from tears, and my feet from falling.**

**116:9 I will walk before the LORD in the land of the living.**

**116:10 I believed, therefore have I spoken: I was greatly afflicted:**

**116:11** I said in my haste, All men are liars.

**116:12** What shall I render unto the LORD for all his benefits toward me?

**116:13** I will take the cup of salvation, and call upon the name of the LORD.

**116:14** I will pay my vows unto the LORD now in the presence of all his people.

**116:15** Precious in the sight of the LORD is the death of his saints.

**116:16** O LORD, truly I am thy servant; I am thy servant, and the son of thine handmaid: thou hast loosed my bonds.

**116:17 I will offer to thee the sacrifice of thanksgiving, and will call upon the name of the LORD.**

**116:18 I will pay my vows unto the LORD now in the presence of all his people.**

**116:19 In the courts of the LORD's house, in the midst of thee,**

**O Jerusalem. Praise ye the LORD.**

**Psalm 118**  **4Q84 & 11Q5 & 11Q6**

**Psalm 118:1 O give thanks unto the LORD; for he is good: because his mercy endureth for ever.**

**118:2 Let Israel now say, that his mercy endureth for ever.**

**118:3 Let the house of Aaron now say, that his mercy endureth for ever.**

118:4 Let them now that fear the LORD say, that his mercy endureth for ever.

118:5 I called upon the LORD in distress: the LORD answered me, and set me in a large place.

**118:6 The LORD is on my side; I will not fear: what can man do unto me?**

**118:7 The LORD taketh my part with them that help me: therefore shall I see my desire upon them that hate me.**

**118:8 It is better to trust in the LORD than to put confidence in man.**

**118:9 It is better to trust in the LORD than to put confidence in princes.**

**118:10 All nations compassed me about: but in the name of the LORD will I destroy them.**

**118:11 They compassed me about; yea, they compassed me about: but in the name of the LORD I will destroy them.**

118:12 They compassed me about like bees: they are quenched as the fire of thorns: for in the name of the LORD I will destroy them.

118:13 Thou hast thrust sore at me that I might fall: but the LORD helped me.

118:14 The LORD is my strength and song, and is become my salvation.

**118:15 The voice of rejoicing and salvation is in the tabernacles of the righteous: the right hand of the LORD doeth valiantly.**

**118:16 The right hand of the LORD is exalted: the right hand of the LORD doeth valiantly.**

118:17 I shall not die, but live, and declare the works of the LORD.

118:18 The LORD hath chastened me sore: but he hath not given me over unto death.

**118:19** Open to me the gates of righteousness: I will go into them, and I will praise the LORD:

**118:20** This gate of the LORD, into which the righteous shall enter.

**118:21** I will praise thee: for thou hast heard me, and art become my salvation.

**118:22** The stone which the builders refused is become the head stone of the corner.

**118:23 This is the LORD's doing; it is marvellous in our eyes.**

**118:24 This is the day which the LORD hath made; we will rejoice and be glad in it.**

**118:25 Save now, I beseech thee, O LORD: O LORD, I beseech thee, send now prosperity.**

**118:26 Blessed be he that cometh in the name of the LORD: we have blessed you out of the house of the LORD.**

**118:27 God is the LORD, which hath showed us light: bind the sacrifice with cords, even unto the horns of the altar.**

**118:28 Thou art my God, and I will praise thee: thou art my God, I will exalt thee.**

**118:29 O give thanks unto the LORD; for he is good: for his mercy endureth for ever.**

**Psalm 119**          **4Q90 & 4Q89 & 11Q5**

Aleph

**Psalm 119:1 Blessed are the undefiled in the way, who walk in the law of the LORD.**
**119:2 Blessed are they that keep his testimonies, and that seek him with the whole heart.**
**119:3 They also do no iniquity: they walk in his ways.**
**119:4 Thou hast commanded us to keep thy precepts diligently.**
**119:5 O that my ways were directed to keep thy statutes!**
**119:6 Then shall I not be ashamed, when I have respect unto all thy commandments.**
119:7 I will praise thee with uprightness of heart, when I shall have learned thy righteous judgments.
119:8 I will keep thy statutes: O forsake me not utterly.

Beth

119:9 Wherewithal shall a young man cleanse his way? By taking heed thereto according to thy word.
**119:10 With my whole heart have I sought thee: O let me not wander from thy commandments.**
**119:11 Thy word have I hid in mine heart, that I might not sin against thee.**
**119:12 Blessed art thou, O LORD: teach me thy statutes.**
**119:13 With my lips have I declared all the judgments of thy mouth.**
**119:14 I have rejoiced in the way of thy testimonies, as much as in all riches.**
**119:15 I will meditate in thy precepts, and have respect unto thy ways.**
**119:16 I will delight myself in thy statutes: I will not forget thy word.**

## Gimel

**119:17 Deal bountifully with thy servant, that I may live, and keep thy word.**
**119:18 Open thou mine eyes, that I may behold wondrous things out of thy law.**
**119:19 I am a stranger in the earth: hide not thy commandments from me.**
**119:20 My soul breaketh for the longing that it hath unto thy judgments at all times.**
**119:21 Thou hast rebuked the proud that are cursed, which do err from thy commandments.**
**119:22 Remove from me reproach and contempt; for I have kept thy testimonies.**
**119:23 Princes also were seated and did speak against me: but thy servant did meditate in thy statutes.**
**119:24 Thy testimonies also are my delight and my counsellors.**

## Daleth

**119:25 My soul cleaveth unto the dust: quicken thou me according to thy word.**
**119:26 I have declared my ways, and thou heardest me: teach me thy statutes.**
**119:27 Make me to understand the way of thy precepts: so shall I talk of thy wondrous works.**
**119:28 My soul melteth for heaviness: strengthen thou me according unto thy word.**
**119:29** Remove from me the way of lying: and grant me thy law graciously.
**119:30** I have chosen the way of truth: thy judgments have I laid before me.
**119:31** I have stuck unto thy testimonies: O LORD, put me not to shame.

**119:32** I will run the way of thy commandments, when thou shalt enlarge my heart.

He

**119:33** Teach me, O LORD, the way of thy statutes; and I shall keep it unto the end.
**119:34** Give me understanding, and I shall keep thy law; yea, I shall observe it with my whole heart.
**119:35** Make me to go in the path of thy commandments; for therein do I delight.
**119:36** Incline my heart unto thy testimonies, and not to covetousness.
**119:37 Turn away mine eyes from beholding vanity; and quicken thou me in thy way.**
**119:38 Establish thy word unto thy servant, who is devoted to thy reverence.**
**119:39 Turn away my reproach which I fear: for thy judgments are good.**
**119:40 Behold, I have longed after thy precepts: quicken me in thy righteousness.**

Vaw

**119:41 Let thy mercies come also unto me, O LORD, even thy salvation, according to thy word.**
**119:42 So shall I have wherewith to answer him that reproacheth me: for I trust in thy word.**
**119:43 And take not the word of truth utterly out of my mouth; for I have hoped in thy judgments.**
**119:44 So shall I keep thy law continually for ever and ever.**
**119:45 And I will walk at liberty: for I seek thy precepts.**
**119:46 I will speak of thy testimonies also before kings, and will not be ashamed.**
**119:47 And I will delight myself in thy commandments, which I have loved.**

**119:48 My hands also will I lift up unto thy commandments, which I have loved; and I will meditate in thy statutes.**

Zayin

**119:49 Remember the word unto thy servant, upon which thou hast caused me to hope.**
**119:50 This is my comfort in my affliction: for thy word hath quickened me.**
119:51 The proud have had me greatly in derision: yet have I not declined from thy law.
119:52 I remembered thy judgments of old, O LORD; and have comforted myself.
119:53 Horror hath taken hold upon me because of the wicked that forsake thy law.
119:54 Thy statutes have been my songs in the house of my pilgrimage.
119:55 I have remembered thy name, O LORD, in the night, and have kept thy law.
119:56 This I had, because I kept thy precepts.

Cheth

119:57 Thou art my portion, O LORD: I have said that I would keep thy words.
119:58 I intreated thy favour with my whole heart: be merciful unto me according to thy word.
**119:59 I thought on my ways, and turned my feet unto thy testimonies.**
**119:60 I made haste, and delayed not to keep thy commandments.**
**119:61 The bands of the wicked have robbed me: but I have not forgotten thy law.**
**119:62 At midnight I will rise to give thanks unto thee because of thy righteous judgments.**
**119:63 I am a companion of all them that fear thee, and of them**

that keep thy precepts.

**119:64 The earth, O LORD, is full of thy mercy: teach me thy statutes.**

Teth

**119:65 Thou hast dealt well with thy servant, O LORD, according unto thy word.**

**119:66 Teach me good judgment and knowledge: for I have believed thy commandments.**

**119:67 Before I was afflicted I went astray: but now have I kept thy word.**

**119:68 Thou art good, and doest good; teach me thy statutes.**

**119:69 The proud have forged a lie against me: but I will keep thy precepts with my whole heart.**

**119:70 Their heart is as fat as grease; but I delight in thy law.**

**119:71 It is good for me that I have been afflicted; that I might learn thy statutes.**

**119:72 The law of thy mouth is better unto me than thousands of gold and silver.**

Yod

**119:73 Thy hands have made me and fashioned me: give me understanding, that I may learn thy commandments.**

**119:74 They that fear thee will be glad when they see me; because I have hoped in thy word.**

**119:75** I know, O LORD, that thy judgments are right, and that thou in faithfulness hast afflicted me.

**119:76** Let, I pray thee, thy merciful kindness be for my comfort, according to thy word unto thy servant.

**119:77** Let thy tender mercies come unto me, that I may live: for thy law is my delight.

**119:78** Let the proud be ashamed; for they dealt perversely with me without a cause: but I will meditate in thy precepts.

**119:79** Let those that fear thee turn unto me, and those that have known thy testimonies.

**119:80** Let my heart be sound in thy statutes; that I be not ashamed.

## Kaph

**119:81 My soul suffers for thy salvation: but I hope in thy word.**
**119:82 Mine eyes fail for thy word, saying, When wilt thou comfort me?**
**119:83 For I am become like a wineskin in the smoke; yet do I not forget thy statutes.**
**119:84** How many are the days of thy servant? When wilt thou execute judgment on them that persecute me?
**119:85** The proud have digged pits for me, which are not after thy law.
**119:86** All thy commandments are faithful: they persecute me wrongfully; help thou me.
**119:87** They had almost consumed me upon earth; but I forsook not thy precepts.
**119:88** Quicken me after thy lovingkindness; so shall I keep the testimony of thy mouth.

## Lamed

**119:89 For ever, O LORD, thy word is settled in heaven.**
**119:90 Thy faithfulness is unto all generations: thou hast established the earth, and it abideth.**
**119:91 They continue this day according to thine ordinances: for all are thy servants.**
**119:92 Unless thy law had been my delights, I should then have perished in mine affliction.**
**119:93 I will never forget thy precepts: for with them thou hast quickened me.**
**119:94 I am thine, save me: for I have sought thy precepts.**
**119:95 The wicked have waited for me to destroy me: but I will consider thy testimonies.**
**119:96 I have seen an end of all perfection: but thy**

**commandment is exceeding broad.**

## Mem

**119:97** O how I love thy law! It is my meditation all the day.
**119:98** Thou through thy commandments hast made me wiser than mine enemies: for they are ever with me.
**119:99** I have more understanding than all my teachers: for thy testimonies are my meditation.
**119:100** I understand more than the ancients, because I keep thy precepts.
**119:101** I have refrained my feet from every evil way, that I might keep thy word.
**119:102** I have not departed from thy judgments: for thou hast taught me.
**119:103** How sweet are thy words unto my taste! Yea, sweeter than honey to my mouth!
**119:104** Through thy precepts I get understanding: therefore I hate every false way.

## Nun

**119:105 Thy word is a lamp unto my feet, and a light unto my path.**
**119:106 I have sworn, and I will perform it, that I will keep thy righteous judgments.**
**119:107 I am afflicted very much: quicken me, O LORD, according unto thy word.**
**119:108 Accept, I beseech thee, the freewill offerings of my mouth, O LORD, and teach me thy judgments.**
**119:109 My soul is continually in my hand: yet do I not forget thy law.**
**119:110 The wicked have laid a snare for me: yet I erred not from thy precepts.**
**119:111 Thy testimonies have I taken as an heritage for ever: for they are the rejoicing of my heart.**

**119:112 I have inclined mine heart to perform thy statutes always, even unto the end.**

Samekh

**119:113 I hate vain thoughts: but thy law do I love.**
**119:114 Thou art my hiding place and my shield: I hope in thy word.**
**119:115 Depart from me, ye evildoers: for I will keep the commandments of my God.**
**119:116 Uphold me according unto thy word, that I may live: and let me not be ashamed of my hope.**
**119:117 Hold thou me up, and I shall be safe: and I will have respect unto thy statutes continually.**
**119:118 Thou hast trodden down all them that err from thy statutes: for their deceit is falsehood.**
**119:119 Thou puts away all the wicked of the earth like dross: therefore I love thy testimonies.**
**119:120 My flesh trembleth for fear of thee; and I am afraid of thy judgments.**

Ayin

**119:121** I have done judgment and justice: leave me not to mine oppressors.
**119:122** Be surety for thy servant for good: let not the proud oppress me.
**119:123** Mine eyes fail for thy salvation, and for the word of thy righteousness.
**119:124** Deal with thy servant according unto thy mercy, and teach me thy statutes.
**119:125** I am thy servant; give me understanding, that I may know thy testimonies.
**119:126** It is time for thee, LORD, to work: for they have made void thy law.
**119:127** Therefore I love thy commandments above gold; yea,

above fine gold.

119:128 Therefore I esteem all thy precepts concerning all things to be right; and I hate every false way.

Pe

119:129 Thy testimonies are wonderful: therefore doth my soul keep them.

119:130 The entrance of thy words giveth light; it giveth understanding unto the simple.

119:131 I opened my mouth, and panted: for I longed for thy commandments.

119:132 Look thou upon me, and be merciful unto me, as thou uses to do unto those that love thy name.

119:133 Order my steps in thy word: and let not any iniquity have dominion over me.

119:134 Deliver me from the oppression of man: so will I keep thy precepts.

119:135 Make thy face to shine upon thy servant; and teach me thy statutes.

119:136 Rivers of waters run down mine eyes, because they keep not thy law.

Tsadde

119:137 Righteous art thou, O LORD, and upright are thy judgments.

119:138 Thy testimonies that thou hast commanded are righteous and very faithful.

119:139 My zeal hath consumed me, because mine enemies have forgotten thy words.

119:140 Thy word is very pure: therefore thy servant loveth it.

119:141 I am small and despised: yet do not I forget thy precepts.

119:142 Thy righteousness is an everlasting righteousness, and thy law is the truth.

**119:143** Trouble and anguish have taken hold on me: yet thy commandments are my delights.
**119:144** The righteousness of thy testimonies is everlasting: give me understanding, and I shall live.

## Qoph

**119:145** I cried with my whole heart; hear me, O LORD: I will keep thy statutes.
**119:146** I cried unto thee; save me, and I shall keep thy testimonies.
**119:147** I met the dawning of the morning, and cried: I hoped in thy word.
**119:148** Mine eyes meet the night watches, that I might meditate in thy word.
**119:149** Hear my voice according unto thy lovingkindness: O LORD, quicken me according to thy judgment.
**119:150 They draw nigh that follow after mischief: they are far from thy law.**
**119:151 Thou art near, O LORD; and all thy commandments are truth.**
**119:152 Concerning thy testimonies, I have known of old that thou hast founded them for ever.**

## Resh

**119:153 Consider mine affliction, and deliver me: for I do not forget thy law.**
**119:154 Plead my cause, and deliver me: quicken me according to thy word.**
**119:155 Salvation is far from the wicked: for they seek not thy statutes.**
**119:156 Great are thy tender mercies, O LORD: quicken me according to thy judgments.**
**119:157 Many are my persecutors and mine enemies; yet do I not decline from thy testimonies.**
**119:158 I beheld the transgressors, and was grieved; because**

they kept not thy word.

**119:159 Consider how I love thy precepts: quicken me, O LORD, according to thy lovingkindness.**

**119:160 Thy word is true from the beginning: and every one of thy righteous judgments endureth for ever.**

## Shin

**119:161 Princes have persecuted me without a cause: but my heart standeth in awe of thy word.**

**119:162 I rejoice at thy word, as one that findeth great plunder.**

**119:163 I hate and abhor lying: but thy law do I love.**

**119:164 Seven times a day do I praise thee because of thy righteous judgments.**

**119:165** Great peace have they which love thy law: and nothing shall offend them.

**119:166** LORD, I have hoped for thy salvation, and done thy commandments.

**119:167** My soul hath kept thy testimonies; and I love them exceedingly.

**119:168** I have kept thy precepts and thy testimonies: for all my ways are before thee.

## Tau

**119:169** Let my cry come near before thee, O LORD: give me understanding according to thy word.

**119:170** Let my supplication come before thee: deliver me according to thy word.

**119:171 My lips shall utter praise, when thou hast taught me thy statutes.**

**119:172 My tongue shall speak of thy word: for all thy commandments are righteousness.**

**119:173 Let thine hand help me; for I have chosen thy precepts.**

**119:174 I have longed for thy salvation, O LORD; and thy law is my delight.**

**119:175 Let my soul live, and it shall praise thee; and let thy judgments help me.**
**119:176 I have gone astray like a lost sheep; seek thy servant; for I do not forget thy commandments.**

**Psalm 120**                  **4Q87**

**Psalm 120:1** In my distress I cried unto the LORD, and he heard me.

**120:2** Deliver my soul, O LORD, from lying lips, and from a deceitful tongue.

**120:3** What shall be given unto thee? Or what shall be done unto thee, thou false tongue?

**120:4** Sharp arrows of the mighty, with coals of juniper.

**120:5** Woe is me, that I sojourn in Mesech, that I dwell in the tents of Kedar!

**120:6 My soul hath long dwelt with him that hateth peace.**

**120:7 I am for peace: but when I speak, they are for war.**

**Psalm 121**            **11Q5**

**Psalm 121:1 I will lift up mine eyes unto the hills, from whence cometh my help.**
**121:2 My help cometh from the LORD, which made heaven and earth.**
**121:3 He will not suffer thy foot to be moved: he that keepeth thee will not slumber.**
**121:4 Behold, he that keepeth Israel shall neither slumber nor sleep.**
**121:5 The LORD is thy keeper: the LORD is thy shade upon thy right hand.**
**121:6 The sun shall not smite thee by day, nor the moon by night.**
**121:7 The LORD shall preserve thee from all evil: he shall preserve thy soul.**
**121:8 The LORD shall preserve thy going out and thy coming in from this time forth, and even for evermore.**

**Psalm 122**     **11Q5**

**Psalm 122:1 I was glad when they said unto me, Let us go into the house of the LORD.**
**122:2 Our feet shall stand within thy gates, O Jerusalem.**
**122:3 Jerusalem is builded as a city that is compact together:**
**122:4 Whither the tribes go up, the tribes of the LORD, unto the testimony of Israel, to give thanks unto the name of the LORD.**
**122:5 For there are set thrones of judgment, the thrones of the house of David.**
**122:6 Pray for the peace of Jerusalem: they shall prosper that love thee.**
**122:7 Peace be within thy walls, and prosperity within thy palaces.**
**122:8 For my brethren and companions' sakes, I will now say, Peace be within thee.**
**122:9 Because of the house of the LORD our God I will seek thy good.**

**Psalm 123**     **11Q5**

**Psalm 123:1 Unto thee lift I up mine eyes, O thou that dwellest in the heavens.**
**123:2 Behold, as the eyes of servants look unto the hand of their masters, and as the eyes of a maiden unto the hand of her mistress; so our eyes wait upon the LORD our God, until that he have mercy upon us.**
**123:3** Have mercy upon us, O LORD, have mercy upon us: for we are exceedingly filled with contempt.
**123:4** Our soul is exceedingly filled with the scorning of those that are at ease, and with the contempt of the proud.

**Psalm 124**          **11Q5**

**Psalm 124:1** If it had not been the LORD who was on our side, now may Israel say;
**124:2** If it had not been the LORD who was on our side, when men rose up against us:
**124:3** Then they had swallowed us up quick, when their wrath was kindled against us:
**124:4** Then the waters had overwhelmed us, the stream had gone over our soul:
**124:5** Then the proud waters had gone over our soul.
**124:6** Blessed be the LORD, who hath not given us as a prey to their teeth.
**124:7** Our soul is escaped as a bird out of the snare of the fowlers: the snare is broken, and we are escaped.
**124:8 Our help is in the name of the LORD, who made heaven and earth.**

**Psalm 125**          **11Q5 & 4Q87**

**Psalm 125:1 They that trust in the LORD shall be as mount Zion, which cannot be removed, but abideth for ever.**
**125:2 As the mountains are round about Jerusalem, so the LORD is round about his people from henceforth even for ever.**
**125:3 For the rod of the wicked shall not rest upon the lot of the righteous; lest the righteous put forth their hands unto iniquity.**
**125:4 Do good, O LORD, unto those that be good, and to them that are upright in their hearts.**
**125:5 As for such as turn aside unto their crooked ways, the LORD shall lead them forth with the workers of iniquity: but peace shall be upon Israel.**

**Psalm 126**           **11Q5 & 4Q87**

**Psalm 126:1 When the LORD turned again the captivity of Zion, we were like them that dream.**
**126:2 Then was our mouth filled with laughter, and our tongue with singing: then said they among the nations, The LORD hath done great things for them.**
**126:3 The LORD hath done great things for us; whereof we are glad.**
**126:4 Turn again our captivity, O LORD, as the streams in the south.**
**126:5 They that sow in tears shall reap in joy.**
**126:6 He that goeth forth and weepeth, bearing precious seed, shall doubtless come again with rejoicing, bringing his sheaves with him.**

**Psalm 127**           **11Q5**

**Psalm 127:1 Except the LORD build the house, they labour in vain that build it: except the LORD keep the city, the watchman waketh but in vain.**
**127:2** It is vain for you to rise up early, to be seated up late, to eat the bread of sorrows: for so he giveth his beloved sleep.
**127:3** Lo, children are an heritage of the LORD: and the fruit of the womb is his reward.
**127:4** As arrows are in the hand of a mighty man; so are children of the youth.
**127:5** Happy is the man that hath his quiver full of them: they shall not be ashamed, but they shall speak with the enemies in the gate.

**Psalm 128**        **11Q5**

**Psalm 128:1** Blessed is every one that feareth the LORD; that walketh in his ways.
**128:2** For thou shalt eat the labour of thine hands: happy shalt thou be, and it shall be well with thee.
**128:3** Thy wife shall be as a fruitful vine by the sides of thine house: thy children like olive plants round about thy table.
**128:4 Behold, that thus shall the man be blessed that feareth the LORD.**
**128:5 The LORD shall bless thee out of Zion: and thou shalt see the good of Jerusalem all the days of thy life.**
**128:6 Yea, thou shalt see thy children's children, and peace upon Israel.**

**Psalm 129**        **11Q5**

**Psalm 129:1 Many a time have they afflicted me from my youth, may Israel now say:**
**129:2 Many a time have they afflicted me from my youth: yet they have not prevailed against me.**
**129:3 The plowers plowed upon my back: they made long their furrows.**
**129:4 The LORD is righteous: he hath cut asunder the cords of the wicked.**
**129:5 Let them all be confounded and turned back that hate Zion.**
**129:6 Let them be as the grass upon the housetops, which withereth afore it groweth up:**
**129:7 Wherewith the mower filleth not his hand; nor he that bindeth sheaves his bosom.**
**129:8 Neither do they which go by say, The blessing of the LORD be upon you: we bless you in the name of the LORD.**

Psalm 130          11Q5 & 4Q87

Psalm 130:1 Out of the depths have I cried unto thee, O LORD.
130:2 Lord, hear my voice: let thine ears be attentive to the voice of my supplications.
130:3 If thou, LORD, shouldest mark iniquities, O Lord, who shall stand?
130:4 But there is forgiveness with thee, that thou mayest be feared.
130:5 I wait for the LORD, my soul doth wait, and in his word do I hope.
130:6 My soul waiteth for the Lord more than they that watch for the morning: I say, more than they that watch for the morning.
130:7 Let Israel hope in the LORD: for with the LORD there is mercy, and with him is plenteous redemption.
130:8 And he shall redeem Israel from all his iniquities.

Psalm 131          11Q5

Psalm 131:1 Lord, my heart is not haughty, nor mine eyes lofty: neither do I exercise myself in great matters, or in things too high for me.
131:2 Surely I have behaved and quieted myself, as a child that is weaned of his mother: my soul is even as a weaned child.
131:3 Let Israel hope in the LORD from henceforth and for ever.

**Psalm 132**         **11Q5**

**Psalm 132:1** Lord, remember David, and all his afflictions:
**132:2** How he sware unto the LORD, and vowed unto the mighty God of Jacob;
**132:3** Surely I will not come into the tabernacle of my house, nor go up into my bed;
**132:4** I will not give sleep to mine eyes, or slumber to mine eyelids,
**132:5** Until I find out a place for the LORD, an habitation for the mighty God of Jacob.
**132:6** Lo, we heard of it at Ephratah: we found it in the fields of the wood.
**132:7** We will go into his tabernacles: we will worship at his footstool.
**132:8 Arise, O LORD, into thy rest; thou, and the ark of thy strength.**
**132:9 Let thy priests be clothed with righteousness; and let thy saints shout for joy.**
**132:10 For thy servant David's sake turn not away the face of thine anointed.**
**132:11 The LORD hath sworn in truth unto David; he will not turn from it; Of the fruit of thy body will I set upon thy throne.**
**132:12 If thy children will keep my covenant and my testimony that I shall teach them, their children shall also be seated upon thy throne for evermore.**
**132:13 For the LORD hath chosen Zion; he hath desired it for his habitation.**
**132:14 This is my rest for ever: here will I dwell; for I have desired it.**
**132:15 I will abundantly bless her provision: I will satisfy her poor with bread.**
**132:16 I will also clothe her priests with salvation: and her saints shall shout aloud for joy.**
**132:17 There will I make the horn of David to bud: I have ordained a lamp for mine anointed.**
**132:18 His enemies will I clothe with shame: but upon himself**

shall his crown flourish.


**Psalm 133          11Q5 & 11Q6**

Psalm 133:1 Behold, how good and how pleasant it is for
brethren to dwell together in unity!
133:2 It is like the precious ointment upon the head, that ran
down upon the beard, even Aaron's beard: that went down to
the skirts of his garments;
133:3 As the dew of Hermon, and as the dew that descended
upon the mountains of Zion: for there the LORD commanded
the blessing, even life for evermore.


**Psalm 134          11Q5**

Psalm 134:1 Behold, bless ye the LORD, all ye servants of the
LORD, which by night stand in the house of the LORD.
134:2 Lift up your hands in the sanctuary, and bless the LORD.
134:3 The LORD that made heaven and earth bless thee out of
Zion.

**Psalm 135**         **4Q95 & 4Q92 & 11Q5**

**Psalm 135:1** Praise ye the LORD. Praise ye the name of the LORD; praise him, O ye servants of the LORD.

**135:2** Ye that stand in the house of the LORD, in the courts of the house of our God.

**135:3** Praise the LORD; for the LORD is good: sing praises unto his name; for it is pleasant.

**135:4** For the LORD hath chosen Jacob unto himself, and Israel for his peculiar treasure.

**135:5** For I know that the LORD is great, and that our Lord is above all gods.

**135:6 Whatsoever the LORD pleased, that did he in heaven, and in earth, in the seas, and all deep places.**

**135:7 He causeth the vapours to ascend from the ends of the earth; he maketh lightnings for the rain; he bringeth the wind out of his treasuries.**

**135:8 Who smote the firstborn of Egypt, both of man and beast.**

**135:9 Who sent tokens and wonders into the midst of thee, O Egypt, upon Pharaoh, and upon all his servants.**

**135:10 Who smote great nations, and slew mighty kings;**

**135:11 Sihon king of the Amorites, and Og king of Bashan, and all the kingdoms of Canaan:**

**135:12 And gave their land for an heritage, an heritage unto Israel his people.**

**135:13 Thy name, O LORD, endureth for ever; and thy memorial, O LORD, throughout all generations.**

**135:14 For the LORD will judge his people, and he will have compassion himself concerning his servants.**

**135:15 The idols of the nations are silver and gold, the work of men's hands.**

**135:16 They have mouths, but they speak not; eyes have they, but they see not;**

**135:17 They have ears, but they hear not; neither is there any breath in their mouths.**

**135:18 They that make them are like unto them: so is every one**

that trusteth in them.

**135:19 Bless the LORD, O house of Israel: bless the LORD, O house of Aaron:**

**135:20 Bless the LORD, O house of Levi: ye that fear the LORD, bless the LORD.**

**135:21 Blessed be the LORD out of Zion, which dwelleth at Jerusalem. Praise ye the LORD.**

**Psalm 136**          **11Q5**

**Psalm 136:1 O give thanks unto the LORD; for he is good: for his mercy endureth for ever.**
**136:2 O give thanks unto the God of gods: for his mercy endureth for ever.**
**136:3 O give thanks to the Lord of lords: for his mercy endureth for ever.**
**136:4 To him who alone doeth great wonders: for his mercy endureth for ever.**
**136:5 To him that by wisdom made the heavens: for his mercy endureth for ever.**
**136:6 To him that stretched out the earth above the waters: for his mercy endureth for ever.**
**136:7 To him that made great lights: for his mercy endureth for ever:**
**136:8 The sun to rule by day: for his mercy endureth for ever:**
**136:9 The moon and stars to rule by night: for his mercy endureth for ever.**
**136:10 To him that smote Egypt in their firstborn: for his mercy endureth for ever:**
**136:11 And brought out Israel from among them: for his mercy endureth for ever:**
**136:12 With a strong hand, and with a stretched out arm: for his mercy endureth for ever.**
**136:13 To him which divided the Red sea into parts: for his mercy endureth for ever:**
**136:14 And made Israel to pass through the midst of it: for his mercy endureth for ever:**
**136:15 But overthrew Pharaoh and his army in the Red sea: for his mercy endureth for ever.**
**136:16 To him which led his people through the wilderness: for his mercy endureth for ever.**
136:17 To him which smote great kings: for his mercy endureth for ever:
136:18 And slew famous kings: for his mercy endureth for ever:

**136:19** Sihon king of the Amorites: for his mercy endureth for ever:
**136:20** And Og the king of Bashan: for his mercy endureth for ever:
**136:21** And gave their land for an heritage: for his mercy endureth for ever:
**136:22** Even an heritage unto Israel his servant: for his mercy endureth for ever.
**136:23** Who remembered us in our low estate: for his mercy endureth for ever:
**136:24** And hath redeemed us from our enemies: for his mercy endureth for ever.
**136:25** Who giveth food to all flesh: for his mercy endureth for ever.
**136:26 O give thanks unto the God of heaven: for his mercy endureth for ever.**

**Psalm 138**            **11Q5**

Psalm 138:1 I will praise thee with my whole heart: before the gods will I sing praise unto thee.

138:2 I will worship toward thy holy temple, and praise thy name for thy lovingkindness and for thy truth: for thou hast magnified thy word above all thy name.

138:3 In the day when I cried thou answered me, and strengthened me with strength in my soul.

138:4 All the kings of the earth shall praise thee, O LORD, when they hear the words of thy mouth.

138:5 Yea, they shall sing in the ways of the LORD: for great is the glory of the LORD.

138:6 Though the LORD be high, yet hath he respect unto the lowly: but the proud he knoweth afar off.

138:7 Though I walk in the midst of trouble, thou wilt revive me: thou shalt stretch forth thine hand against the wrath of mine enemies, and thy right hand shall save me.

138:8 The LORD will perfect that which concerneth me: thy mercy, O LORD, endureth for ever: forsake not the works of thine own hands.

**Psalm 139**          **11Q5**

**Psalm 139:1** O lord, thou hast searched me, and known me.
**139:2** Thou knowest when I am seated down and mine rising up, thou understandest my thought afar off.
**139:3** Thou compassest my path and my lying down, and art acquainted with all my ways.
**139:4** For there is not a word in my tongue, but, lo, O LORD, thou knowest it altogether.
**139:5** Thou hast compassed me behind and before, and laid thine hand upon me.
**139:6** Such knowledge is too wonderful for me; it is high, I cannot attain unto it.
**139:7** Whither shall I go from thy spirit? Or whither shall I flee from thy presence?
**139:8 If I ascend up into heaven, thou art there: if I make my bed in hell, behold, thou art there.**
**139:9 If I take the wings of the morning, and dwell in the uttermost parts of the sea;**
**139:10 Even there shall thy hand lead me, and thy right hand shall hold me.**
**139:11 If I say, Surely the darkness shall cover me; even the night shall be light about me.**
**139:12 Yea, the darkness hideth not from thee; but the night shineth as the day: the darkness and the light are both alike to thee.**
**139:13 For thou hast possessed my flesh: thou hast covered me in my mother's womb.**
**139:14 I will praise thee; for I am fearfully and wonderfully made: marvellous are thy works; and that my soul knoweth right well.**
**139:15 My substance was not hid from thee, when I was made in secret, and curiously wrought in the lowest parts of the earth.**
**139:16 Thine eyes did see my substance, yet being uncompleted; and in thy book all my members were written, which in continuance were fashioned, when as yet there was none of**

them.
139:17 How precious also are thy thoughts unto me, O God! How great is the sum of them!
139:18 If I should count them, they are more in number than the sand: when I awake, I am still with thee.
139:19 Surely thou wilt slay the wicked, O God: depart from me therefore, ye bloody men.
139:20 For they speak against thee wickedly, and thine enemies take thy name in vain.
139:21 Do not I hate them, O LORD, that hate thee? And am not I grieved with those that rise up against thee?
139:22 I hate them with perfect hatred: I count them mine enemies.
139:23 Search me, O God, and know my heart: try me, and know my thoughts:
139:24 And see if there be any wicked way in me, and lead me in the way everlasting.

## Psalm 141          11Q5

**Psalm 141:1** Lord, I cry unto thee: make haste unto me; give ear unto my voice, when I cry unto thee.

**141:2** Let my prayer be set forth before thee as incense; and the lifting up of my hands as the evening sacrifice.

**141:3** Set a watch, O LORD, before my mouth; keep the door of my lips.

**141:4** Incline not my heart to any evil thing, to practise wicked works with men that work iniquity: and let me not eat of their delicacies.

**141:5 Let the righteous smite me; it shall be a kindness: and let him reprove me; it shall be an excellent oil, which shall not break my head: for yet my prayer also shall be in their calamities.**

**141:6 When their judges are overthrown in stony places, they shall hear my words; for they are sweet.**

**141:7 Our bones are scattered at the grave's mouth, as when one cutteth and cleaveth wood upon the earth.**

**141:8 But mine eyes are unto thee, O GOD the Lord: in thee is my trust; leave not my soul destitute.**

**141:9 Keep me from the snares which they have laid for me, and the gins of the workers of iniquity.**

**141:10 Let the wicked fall into their own nets, whilst that I withal escape.**

## Psalm 142         11Q5

**Psalm 142:1** I cried unto the LORD with my voice; with my voice unto the LORD did I make my supplication.

**142:2** I poured out my complaint before him; I showed before him my trouble.

**142:3 When my spirit was overwhelmed within me, then thou knewest my path. In the way wherein I walked have they privily laid a snare for me.**

**142:4 I looked on my right hand, and beheld, but there was no man that would know me: refuge failed me; no man cared for my soul.**

**142:5 I cried unto thee, O LORD: I said, Thou art my refuge and my portion in the land of the living.**

**142:6 Attend unto my cry; for I am brought very low: deliver me from my persecutors; for they are stronger than I.**

**142:7 Bring my soul out of prison, that I may praise thy name: the righteous shall compass me about; for thou shalt deal bountifully with me.**

**Psalm 143**  **11Q5**

**Psalm 143:1 Hear my prayer, O LORD, give ear to my supplications: in thy faithfulness answer me, and in thy righteousness.**
**143:2 And enter not into judgment with thy servant: for in thy sight shall no man living be justified.**
**143:3 For the enemy hath persecuted my soul; he hath stricken my life down to the ground; he hath made me to dwell in darkness, as those that have been long dead.**
**143:4 Therefore is my spirit overwhelmed within me; my heart within me is desolate.**
**143:5 I remember the days of old; I meditate on all thy works; I muse on the work of thy hands.**
**143:6 I stretch forth my hands unto thee: my soul thirsteth after thee, as a thirsty land. Selah.**
**143:7 Hear me speedily, O LORD: my spirit faileth: hide not thy face from me, lest I be like unto them that go down into the pit.**
**143:8 Cause me to hear thy lovingkindness in the morning; for in thee do I trust: cause me to know the way wherein I should walk; for I lift up my soul unto thee.**
**143:9** Deliver me, O LORD, from mine enemies: I flee unto thee to hide me.
**143:10** Teach me to do thy will; for thou art my God: thy spirit is good; lead me into the land of uprightness.
**143:11** Quicken me, O LORD, for thy name's sake: for thy righteousness' sake bring my soul out of trouble.
**143:12** And of thy mercy cut off mine enemies, and destroy all them that afflict my soul: for I am thy servant.

**Psalm 144**                    **11Q5**

**Psalm 144:1 Blessed be the LORD my strength which teacheth my hands to war, and my fingers to fight:**
**144:2 My goodness, and my fortress; my high tower, and my deliverer; my shield, and he in whom I trust; who subdueth my people under me.**
**144:3 LORD, what is man, that thou takest knowledge of him! Or the son of man, that thou makest account of him!**
**144:4 Man is like to vanity: his days are as a shadow that passeth away.**
**144:5 Bow thy heavens, O LORD, and come down: touch the mountains, and they shall smoke.**
**144:6 Cast forth lightning, and scatter them: shoot out thine arrows, and destroy them.**
**144:7 Send thine hand from above; rid me, and deliver me out of great waters, from the hand of strange children;**
**144:8** Whose mouth speaketh vanity, and their right hand is a right hand of falsehood.
**144:9** I will sing a new song unto thee, O God: upon a psaltery and an instrument of ten strings will I sing praises unto thee.
**144:10** It is he that giveth salvation unto kings: who delivereth David his servant from the hurtful sword.
**144:11** Rid me, and deliver me from the hand of strange children, whose mouth speaketh vanity, and their right hand is a right hand of falsehood:
**144:12** That our sons may be as plants grown up in their youth; that our daughters may be as corner stones, polished after the similitude of a palace:
**144:13** That our garners may be full, affording all manner of store: that our sheep may bring forth thousands and ten thousands in our streets:
**144:14** That our oxen may be strong to labour; that there be no breaking in, nor going out; that there be no complaining in our streets.
**144:15 Happy is that people, that is in such a case: yea, happy is**

**that people, whose God is the LORD.**

## Psalm 145          11Q5

**Psalm 145:1** I will extol thee, my God, O king; and I will bless thy name for ever and ever.

**145:2** Every day will I bless thee; and I will praise thy name for ever and ever.

**145:3** Great is the LORD, and greatly to be praised; and his greatness is unsearchable.

**145:4** One generation shall praise thy works to another, and shall declare thy mighty acts.

**145:5** I will speak of the glorious honour of thy majesty, and of thy wondrous works.

**145:6** And men shall speak of the might of thy awesome acts: and I will declare thy greatness.

**145:7** They shall abundantly utter the memory of thy great goodness, and shall sing of thy righteousness.

**145:8** The LORD is gracious, and full of compassion; slow to anger, and of great mercy.

**145:9** The LORD is good to all: and his tender mercies are over all his works.

**145:10** All thy works shall praise thee, O LORD; and thy saints shall bless thee.

**145:11** They shall speak of the glory of thy kingdom, and talk of thy power;

**145:12** To make known to the sons of men his mighty acts, and the glorious majesty of his kingdom.

**145:13 Thy kingdom is an everlasting kingdom, and thy dominion endureth throughout all generations.**

**145:14 The LORD upholdeth all that fall, and raiseth up all those that be bowed down.**

**145:15 The eyes of all wait upon thee; and thou givest them their food in due season.**

**145:16 Thou openest thine hand, and satisfiest the desire of every living thing.**

**145:17 The LORD is righteous in all his ways, and holy in all his works.**

**145:18 The LORD is nigh unto all them that call upon him, to all that call upon him in truth.**
**145:19 He will fulfil the desire of them that fear him: he also will hear their cry, and will save them.**
**145:20 The LORD preserveth all them that love him: but all the wicked will he destroy.**
**145:21 My mouth shall speak the praise of the LORD: and let all flesh bless his holy name for ever and ever.**

**Psalm 146          11Q5**

Psalm 146:1 Praise ye the LORD. Praise the LORD, O my soul.
146:2 While I live will I praise the LORD: I will sing praises unto my God while I have any being.
146:3 Put not your trust in princes, nor in the son of man, in whom there is no help.
146:4 His breath goeth forth, he returneth to his earth; in that very day his thoughts perish.
146:5 Happy is he that hath the God of Jacob for his help, whose hope is in the LORD his God:
146:6 Which made heaven, and earth, the sea, and all that therein is: which keepeth truth for ever:
146:7 Which executeth judgment for the oppressed: which giveth food to the hungry. The LORD lets loose the prisoners:
146:8 The LORD openeth the eyes of the blind: the LORD raiseth them that are bowed down: the LORD loveth the righteous:
**146:9 The LORD preserveth the strangers; he relieveth the fatherless and widow: but the way of the wicked he turneth upside down.**
**146:10 The LORD shall reign for ever, even thy God, O Zion, unto all generations. Praise ye the LORD.**

**Psalm 147**         **11Q5**

**Psalm 147:1 Praise ye the LORD: for it is good to sing praises unto our God; for it is pleasant; and praise is comely.**
**147:2 The LORD doth build up Jerusalem: he gathereth together the outcasts of Israel.**
**147:3 He healeth the broken in heart, and bindeth up their wounds.**
147:4 He telleth the number of the stars; he calleth them all by their names.
147:5 Great is our Lord, and of great power: his understanding is infinite.
147:6 The LORD lifteth up the meek: he casteth the wicked down to the ground.
147:7 Sing unto the LORD with thanksgiving; sing praise upon the harp unto our God:
147:8 Who covereth the heaven with clouds, who prepareth rain for the earth, who maketh grass to grow upon the mountains.
147:9 He giveth to the beast his food, and to the young ravens which cry.
147:10 He delighteth not in the strength of the horse: he taketh not pleasure in the legs of a man.
147:11 The LORD taketh pleasure in them that fear him, in those that hope in his mercy.
147:12 Praise the LORD, O Jerusalem; praise thy God, O Zion.
147:13 For he hath strengthened the bars of thy gates; he hath blessed thy children within thee.
147:14 He maketh peace in thy borders, and filleth thee with the finest of the wheat.
147:15 He sendeth forth his commandment upon earth: his word runneth very swiftly.
147:16 He giveth snow like wool: he scattereth the hoarfrost like ashes.
147:17 He casteth forth his ice like morsels: who can stand before his cold?
**147:18 He sendeth out his word, and melteth them: he causeth**

his wind to blow, and the waters flow.

147:19 He showeth his word unto Jacob, his statutes and his judgments unto Israel.

147:20 He hath not dealt so with any nation: and as for his judgments, they have not known them. Praise ye the LORD.

**Psalm 148**          **11Q5**

**Psalm 148:1 Praise ye the LORD. Praise ye the LORD from the heavens: praise him in the heights.**
**148:2 Praise ye him, all his angels: praise ye him, all his armies.**
**148:3 Praise ye him, sun and moon: praise him, all ye stars of light.**
**148:4 Praise him, ye heavens of heavens, and ye waters that be above the heavens.**
**148:5 Let them praise the name of the LORD: for he commanded, and they were created.**
**148:6 He hath also established them for ever and ever: he hath made a decree which shall not pass away.**
**148:7 Praise the LORD from the earth, ye dragons, and all deeps:**
**148:8 Fire, and hail; snow, and vapours; stormy wind fulfilling his word:**
**148:9 Mountains, and all hills; fruitful trees, and all cedars:**
**148:10 Beasts, and all cattle; roaming things, and flying fowl:**
**148:11 Kings of the earth, and all people; princes, and all judges of the earth:**
**148:12 Both young men, and maidens; old men, and children:**
148:13 Let them praise the name of the LORD: for his name alone is excellent; his glory is above the earth and heaven.
148:14 He also exalteth the horn of his people, the praise of all his saints; even of the children of Israel, a people near unto him. Praise ye the LORD.

**Psalm 149**　　　　　**11Q5**

**Psalm 149:1** Praise ye the LORD. Sing unto the LORD a new song, and his praise in the congregation of saints.
**149:2** Let Israel rejoice in him that made him: let the children of Zion be joyful in their King.
**149:3** Let them praise his name in the dance: let them sing praises unto him with the timbrel and harp.
**149:4** For the LORD taketh pleasure in his people: he will beautify the meek with salvation.
**149:5** Let the saints be joyful in glory: let them sing aloud upon their beds.
**149:6** Let the high praises of God be in their mouth, and a two-edged sword in their hand;
**149:7** To execute vengeance upon the nations, and punishments upon the people;
**149:8** To bind their kings with chains, and their nobles with fetters of iron;
**149:9 To execute upon them the judgment written: this honour have all his saints. Praise ye the LORD.**

**Psalm 150**                    **11Q5**

**Psalm 150:1 Praise ye the LORD. Praise God in his sanctuary: praise him in the firmament of his power.**
**150:2 Praise him for his mighty acts: praise him according to his excellent greatness.**
**150:3 Praise him with the sound of the trumpet: praise him with the psaltery and harp.**
**150:4 Praise him with the timbrel and dance: praise him with stringed instruments and organs.**
**150:5 Praise him upon the loud cymbals: praise him upon the high sounding cymbals.**
**150:6 Let every thing that hath breath praise the LORD. Praise ye the LORD.**

Bibliography:

*King James Version Bible*

Martinez, F. G., & Tigchelaar, E. J. C., editors,
*The Dead Sea Scrolls Study Edition,* Vol. 1 & Vol. 2.
(1997, 1998), (2000).

Green, Jay P., Sr., *The Interlinear Bible: Hebrew-Greek-English.*
Second Edition (1986).

# Dead Sea Scrolls Psalms

*
*     *

11211815R10085

Printed in Great Britain
by Amazon